MW01076860

# GOD, WHAT DO I DO?

# GOD, WHAT DO I DO?

## A BIBLE STUDY ON JUDGES 1–5 ABOUT MAKING WISE DECISIONS IN UNCERTAIN TIMES

## KATIE M. REID

BakerBooks
a division of Baker Publishing Group
Grand Rapids, Michigan

© 2025 by Katie M. Reid

Published by Baker Books
a division of Baker Publishing Group
Grand Rapids, Michigan
BakerBooks.com

Printed in the United States of America

All rights reserved. No part of this publication may be reproduced, stored in a retrieval system, or transmitted in any form or by any means—for example, electronic, photocopy, recording—without the prior written permission of the publisher. The only exception is brief quotations in printed reviews.

Library of Congress Cataloging-in-Publication Data
Names: Reid, Katie M., author.
Title: God, what do i do? : a bible study on Judges 1–5 about making wise decisions in uncertain times / Katie M. Reid.
Description: Grand Rapids, Michigan : Baker Books, a division of Baker Publishing Group, [2025]
Identifiers: LCCN 2024038995 | ISBN 9781540904591 (paperback) | ISBN 9781493450435 (ebook)
Subjects: LCSH: Bible. Judges, I–V—Study and teaching. | Christian women—Religious life—Biblical teaching.
Classification: LCC BS1305.55 .R45 2025 | DDC 222/.32—dc23/eng/20241121
LC record available at https://lccn.loc.gov/2024038995

Unless otherwise indicated, Scripture quotations are from the Christian Standard Bible®. Copyright © 2017 by Holman Bible Publishers. Used by permission. Christian Standard Bible® and CSB® are federally registered trademarks of Holman Bible Publishers.

Scripture quotations labeled ESV are from The Holy Bible, English Standard Version® (ESV®). Copyright © 2001 by Crossway, a publishing ministry of Good News Publishers. Used by permission. All rights reserved. ESV Text Edition: 2016

Scripture quotations labeled NIV are from the Holy Bible, New International Version®, NIV®. Copyright © 1973, 1978, 1984, 2011 by Biblica, Inc.® Used by permission of Zondervan. All rights reserved worldwide. www.zondervan.com. The "NIV" and "New International Version" are trademarks registered in the United States Patent and Trademark Office by Biblica, Inc.®

Scripture quotations labeled NLT are from the Holy Bible, New Living Translation. Copyright © 1996, 2004, 2015 by Tyndale House Foundation. Used by permission of Tyndale House Publishers, Carol Stream, Illinois 60188. All rights reserved.

Cover photo by Beth Rubin, B Creative Inspiration.
Author photo by Agapeland Photography.

The author is represented by the literary agency of WTA Media, LLC.

Baker Publishing Group publications use paper produced from sustainable forestry practices and postconsumer waste whenever possible.

25  26  27  28  29  30  31        7  6  5  4  3  2  1

To the women who have helped shaped my faith:
Mom, Sarae, Laurie, Paula, and Christy


For God has not given us a spirit of fear,
but one of power, love, and sound judgment.
2 TIMOTHY 1:7

# Contents

# How to Use This Study

Whether you study the Bible on a regular basis, are an occasional reader, or are brand-new to it, I invite you to read God's Word as loving instructions given to you by a perfect heavenly Father. When you interact with the Bible through the lens of His lavish love, you begin to see the text—and God, others, and yourself—in a different way.

## Perspective Shift

I spent decades living as a slave to God instead of delighting in being a daughter of God. I made decisions out of a place of guilt instead of grace, out of burden instead of freedom, out of fear instead of faith. It was a miserable way to live. I am grateful Jesus delivered me from that crippling mindset and shifted my perspective to enjoy and honor Him instead of wearing myself out trying to impress Him.

I don't want you to fall into that performance trap like I did.

As you go through this study and learn about the judges and the actions they took, invite God to teach you about Himself and to solidify decisions you can make that will serve you well and honor Him in the process.

There are clear commands provided in God's Word for our protection. Like a parent cupping the face of their child, trying to help them understand a better way, God may do the same with us. He is willing to correct us because He wants more for us, like He did for the Israelites during the time of the judges. We may be tempted to bypass difficult passages of

Scripture but, as you will see throughout this study, the gospel is present throughout the entirety of Scripture. Even the hard-to-understand accounts in the Bible point to the character of God and the incredible story of deliverance, redemption, and restoration He offers us through Jesus. It's such Good News!

## The Lay of the Land

Before you begin Week 1, there is an introductory lesson that will lay the foundation for the entire study. Don't skip over this short lesson because it provides a necessary foundation.

Pray before you begin each lesson, asking God to help you understand what you are reading, get to know Him better, and grow in your relationship with Him. A brief overview and a key verse are given before each week of study begins. Those five verses would be great to memorize.

### Lesson Layout

There are five weeks of study and five lessons of study within each week, plus the introductory lesson. Each week begins by stating the overarching decision that frames every lesson. Together, we will learn how to:

- Remember who Jesus is and what He has done.
- Obey God's commands completely, not partially.
- Be responsible with our thoughts, actions, and influence.
- Endure through the power of the Holy Spirit and the armor of God.
- Rise in faith to fulfill our unique purpose at this time in history.
- Testify of God's power, His glorious deeds, and His mighty wonders.

Each day's lesson has five main sections: **Read**, **Focus**, **Engage**, **Reflect**, and **Decide**. The **Read** section introduces the day's Bible passage as well as the main verse for the lesson. Read the Bible passage in its entirety before you start each day of study. Consider reading it out loud to help you stay focused. The **Focus** section includes teaching about the passage to help you interact further with what you have just read. The **Engage** section includes questions, fill in the blanks, matching, and other activities to enrich your study. The **Reflect** section provides an opportunity to apply what you learned through questions designed to lead you to action. And finally, each lesson ends with a **Decide** statement to help you move forward in your faith. Altogether, there are twenty-five decisions offered over the course of this study to empower you as you take your next steps. At the end of each week you will find a prayer and wrap-up questions to summarize what you learned.

Also included in each lesson are **Bonus** study opportunities to help you broaden your knowledge and go deeper into the text. If time allows, feel free to engage with some or all of the bonus content.

Each day's lesson will take about twenty to thirty minutes to complete. Structure your time of study in whatever way works best for you. The point isn't to rush through but to take time to contemplate what God is showing you about Himself, His people, and how you can move forward with godly wisdom in whatever decision you face.

### Which Version of the Bible Should I Use?

The Christian Standard Bible (CSB) is used throughout this study. Some of the fill-in-the-blank questions will be based on the CSB version; if you don't have a copy of the CSB, you can look up the passages on BibleGateway.com or in the YouVersion app.

You can do this study on your own, with a friend, or in a small or large group.

> **Access additional resources, like the key verse printables, further teaching, group resources, and a Bible study playlist, at KatieMReid.com/Judges/.**

I am excited that you have decided to dive into this study!
All In,
Katie

*Dear God,*

*Thank You for the gift of Your Word. Increase our appetite for truth. May we crave time with You and find satisfaction in Your presence. Instead of striving to figure things out, may we surrender more to You. Instead of trying to muster up the desire to study, may we receive Your help to adjust our approach and view Bible study as a "get to," not a "have to."*

*How amazing it is that we can encounter You, the living God! Thank You for this journey through Judges. Teach us what we need to understand and apply to bring You glory and grow up in You. Illuminate Your Word, show us where we have wandered, and lead us back to You—to Your open arms, ready to forgive and receive us.*

*We offer up the areas where we are uncertain, where we aren't sure which way to turn or what to do next. You are waiting to guide us; we simply have to ask. Give us ears to hear, eyes to see, minds to comprehend, and hearts ready to follow Your direction, receive Your loving correction, and apply Your time-tested wisdom for the days ahead.*

*In Jesus's name, Amen.*

# THE DECISION TO REMEMBER

## Mount Precipice

The ascent up the steep hill is slow going in the oven-like heat of the Middle East. One sandaled foot in front of the other, I step closer to the top. Finally, I reach the stone-capped platform and am privy to a panoramic view of the Jezreel Valley. Like a bird of prey, I scan the horizon for my prize. The small town of Nazareth, peppered with slate gray buildings, comes into focus.

I can almost hear a cinematic soundtrack converging upon this moment, the orchestra's score swelling across the desert landscape as it reaches Mount Precipice. I imagine a sweeping aerial shot from a drone, circling over the ancient landmark as I, a fortysomething from the middle of Michigan, am close to encountering something I've been greatly anticipating.

Mount Precipice is believed to be the place the Nazareth townies wanted to throw Jesus off a cliff (see Luke 4:28–30). Thankfully, they didn't get their way. "[Jesus] passed right through the crowd and went on his way" (Luke 4:30).

With the patchwork of fertile fields below and Mount Tabor and Mount Gilboa in the distance, our trip's instructor begins talking about a woman from Scripture he has already mentioned numerous times throughout our travels. *Deborah*. Every time he mentioned her, something stirred in my soul. I was compelled to pay close attention.

With the bird's-eye view from Mount Precipice, I take in the scope of the battle that Deborah and Barak led in response to the Lord's command, recorded in Judges 4. Over a thousand years before Jesus was spared from premature destruction near his hometown, as recounted in Luke 4:28–30, and before Jesus delivered us from sin's destruction by dying on the cross, God provided judges, like Deborah, to serve as temporary deliverers to His people. The judges helped the people make wise decisions in a morally corrupt and hostile climate—pointing to their ultimate need for a permanent Deliverer.

Before we navigate our way through Judges 1–5, it is important to understand key components of God's character and His plan to deliver humanity from the bondage of sin and restore us to Himself. The judges were given to provide temporary deliverance to God's people, whose enemies ruled

over them because the people had rebelled against God's clear instructions. Yet the greater purpose of the judges was to point the Israelites, and us as well, to our need for a perfect and complete Deliverer, Jesus Christ, who died and rose to free us from the earthly burden and eternal consequences of sin, once and for all.

Israel's Jezreel Valley, a region repeatedly contested throughout history, serves as the setting for our study in Judges 1–5. The introductory lesson, in the following pages, lays a strong biblical foundation to stand upon as you discover the first wise decision you can make in uncertain times.

# "God, What Do I Do When I'm Unsure?"

But because the L ORD loved you and kept the oath he swore to your ancestors, he brought you out with a strong hand and redeemed you from the place of slavery, from the power of Pharaoh king of Egypt.

DEUTERONOMY 7:8

## Read

DEUTERONOMY 7

What is something you are unsure about? How do you find clarity in times of uncertainty? Throughout this study, you will discover decisions you *can* make even when you aren't sure what to do about a particular situation in your life. The power of remembering is the first guiding principle in making wise decisions. When we remember what has been promised through Scripture, we are less likely to despair when we are unsure about what to do in our own lives. God tells His people to remember who He is, what He has instructed, and what He has done.

## Focus

In order to understand the context and time of Judges, we need to remember what God promised His people in the past and how they arrived at this point in their history.

In Genesis 15, God promised Abram, later renamed Abraham, the following things:

- Abram would have offspring as numerous as the stars (vv. 4–5).
- Abram's offspring would be foreigners for four hundred years in a land that did not belong to them, and they would be enslaved and oppressed (v. 13).
- God would judge the nation that Abram's descendants would serve, and they would go out of that land with many possessions (v. 14).
- Abram would go to his fathers in peace and be buried at a good old age (v. 15).

God outwardly demonstrated His unconditional covenant in Genesis 15:17–21, assuring Abram that He would keep and fulfill the promises He had given him. Clear guidance for Abram's next steps was provided in the bedrock of God's promises.

It is important for us to remember God's covenant with Abraham and the fulfillment of His promises to him and his descendants as we begin our study. Here is a brief flyover: God provided a son, Isaac, to Abraham and his wife, Sarah. Hundreds of years later, Abraham's descendants became as numerous as the stars. God then delivered them out of slavery in Egypt through Moses. God formed the Hebrews into Israel, a nation set apart for Him, during their forty years in the wilderness. He gave them laws to live by. After Moses died, Joshua led the people into the land God had promised to them. Throughout this process, the Israelites made mistakes, they rebelled, and they forgot God's faithfulness time and time again, yet God did not forget His promise to them. God did not break the covenant He made with Abraham and his descendants (Ps. 105:7–11).

The rest of our study takes place after the Israelites entered the land God promised them and started to possess it more fully, through battle.

God had clearly instructed them to drive out the nations living in the land, but they failed to do so, and now the Israelites found themselves needing deliverance from those same nations. Even though they failed in many ways, God did not forget them. He sent temporary judges to govern them, foreshadowing their need for permanent deliverance from the oppression of sin.

## Engage

If you haven't already done so, read Deuteronomy 7, which will help you solidify the covenant God made with His people and better understand Judges 1; then answer the following questions.

1. Verse 1 states that seven nations were to be driven out of the land that was promised to God's people. What were the names of these people groups?

   **H** ethites

   **G**

   **A**

   **C**

   **P**

   **H**

   **J**

2. Write out Deuteronomy 7:2 below:

3. In Deuteronomy 7:3, God instructs His people not to intermarry with these nations. What reason does He give for this in verse 4?

4. At the end of verse 4, God reveals what His response will be if His instructions are disobeyed. Write out His response:

In verse 5, God clearly lays out four directives for His people in regard to the seven nations mentioned in verse 1.

A. Tear down their altars.

B. Smash their sacred pillars.

C. Cut down their Asherah poles (we will discuss these in a coming lesson).

D. Burn their carved images.

Verse 6 gives the "why" to these required actions: "For you are a holy people belonging to the LORD your God. The LORD your God has chosen you to be his own possession out of all the peoples on the face of the earth."

5. Verses 7–8 provide the reasons God chose the Hebrews to be His chosen people. List these reasons below:

### Forget-Me-Not

At the end of Deuteronomy 7:8, we read about God reminding His people that He brought them out from under their oppression in Egypt with His strong hand, redeeming them from slavery and the power of Pharaoh. When we forget what God has done for us in the past, we can be tempted to despair or to slip into arrogance, taking credit for our successes.

The following verses serve as an important warning to the Hebrews and to us when we experience deliverance from oppression and experience the blessing of God's promises.

> Be careful that you don't forget the Lord your God by failing to keep his commands, ordinances, and statutes that I am giving you today. When you eat and are full, and build beautiful houses to live in, and your herds and flocks grow large, and your silver and gold multiply, and everything else you have increases, be careful that your heart doesn't become proud and you forget the Lord your God who brought you out of the land of Egypt, out of the place of slavery. (Deut. 8:11–14)

Remembering what God did in the past helps inform our present and future decisions. God is infinite and all-knowing; He does not forget His promises. The only thing He chooses to forget is the sin of those who are in Christ (Isa. 43:25; Jer. 31:34; Heb. 8:12). Being "in" Christ means believing in Him, that He is who He says He is in the Bible. It involves receiving His salvation by accepting His forgiveness for our sins, following Jesus, and aligning our lives to His will. In essence, it's about being "all in," holding nothing back from Him.

As we take a closer look at some of the temporary judges God raised up, keep in mind that they serve as an arrow pointing forward to the perfect and total deliverance available to us through the death and resurrection of Christ. Throughout the totality of Scripture, we see our desperate need for deliverance and God answering our deepest need with His greatest gift to us. No matter how dark things get, the promise and hope of Jesus is present—from Genesis to Judges, from the Gospels to Revelation. Not only is it important to remember what God has done for His people in the past, it is crucial to remember what Jesus has done for us.

### Jesus's Ta-Da List

Here is a sampling of the incredible things Jesus has already accomplished!

- ☑ Left heaven and came to earth in the flesh (John 1:1–14)
- ☑ Instructed in truth (John 14:5–6)
- ☑ Pointed to the Father (John 14:8–11)
- ☑ Died on the cross for our sins, was buried, rose again (1 Cor. 15:3–4)
- ☑ Took away sins through His sacrifice (John 1:29)
- ☑ Demonstrated His love for us (Rom. 5:8)
- ☑ Showed us how to love others (John 13:34–35)
- ☑ Gave us the Holy Spirit (John 14:15–17)

This is Jesus's faithfulness on display. Not only did He provide all of this—and more—for us but He is coming back again!

It is comforting that God does not forget us (Isa. 49:14–16). He keeps His promises. God upholds His covenant even when we fail. When we are convinced of God's lavish love, it helps us make clearheaded decisions. Could it be that you're having trouble making a decision because you have forgotten that God does not forget you?

Recalling what Jesus has done for us is a necessary practice. It strengthens our faith to remember He is our Promise Keeper and our Ultimate Deliverer. He has gone to prepare a place for us, if we are His.

## Reflect

How do you know if you are His? Read the following verses to find out:

Romans 10:9

2 Timothy 2:19

John 14:5–7

## Bonus

Choose one of the statements from the "Ta-Da" list of Jesus's amazing acts. Look up the corresponding Bible verse(s) listed beside it and read it through. Record what you learn below:

### DECIDE

When you aren't sure what to do, decide to remember that God doesn't forget what He promised His people.

*Dear Jesus,*

*We want to remember how You have redeemed us even though we dirtied ourselves by rebelling against Your pure love for us. You rescued us out of our slavery to sin, giving us new life through Your costly and complete sacrifice for us. You made a way for our sins to be forgiven and our shame to be removed completely. You abolished death and threw down our enemy, the devil, the accuser. We are so grateful. We choose to receive Your deep love for us, proven on the cross, and rely on Your salvation, not our own strength. Help us not to flirt with the world; we want to be faithful to You and have sincere hearts toward You (Ps. 78:22, 42, 34–37). Help us to understand our new identity in You and to behave accordingly, knowing we are loved and cherished—not because we have earned it but because You have mercifully offered that which we have not, and could not, earn.*

*We are your Bride, bought with a price; our value is found in You. Thank You that we have not been left alone. You have given us the gift of Your Holy Spirit to remind us of what You have done and what You have instructed. With great anticipation, we actively await the day when You return for Your Bride and we will experience complete union with You, our Groom. You alone are worthy to receive praise, glory, and honor!*

*In the Name above every name, Amen.*

# WEEKLY WRAP-UP

*This week, I decide to remember who Jesus is and what He has done.*

God promised Abraham he would be the father of many nations and God would give his descendants the land of Canaan (Gen. 17:1–9). Fast-forward a few hundred years, and Moses led the Hebrews (Abraham's offspring) out of their bondage in Egypt and to the Promised Land. Then Moses died (Deut. 34:1–11). Joshua led God's chosen people into the Promised Land and helped them begin to inhabit the land (Josh. 1:1–6). Then Joshua died (24:29–32). There was still work to be done for God's people to fully possess what He promised them. But with their earthly leaders gone, it was time to see if they would do what was right without the oversight they once had.

Answer the following questions to help summarize what you learned during this introductory lesson. If possible, use biblical references to back up your responses.

1. What did God deliver His people from?




2. What did God promise His people?

3. What did Jesus deliver us from?

4. What does Jesus promise us?

5. Based on what you discovered in this introduction, how can the decision to remember help you make wise decisions in uncertain times?

# THE DECISION TO OBEY

## JUDGES 1

Now that we have taken a closer look at God's faithfulness in making and keeping a covenant with Abraham, delivering the Israelites from Egypt, and providing us deliverance from sin and eternal separation from Him through Jesus's death and resurrection, it's time to dig into Judges chapter 1. This week of study will focus on what happened to the Israelites in the Promised Land. As we examine what they did well and what they got wrong, we will discover that the decision to obey God is the best choice we can make, no matter what happens next.

He then took the covenant scroll and read it aloud to the people. They responded, "We will do and obey all that the Lᴏʀᴅ has commanded."

# LESSON 1

# "God, What Do I Do First?"

The LORD answered, "Judah is to go. I have handed the land
over to him."

JUDGES 1:2

## Read

JUDGES 1:1–2

When you are faced with uncertainty, what do you do? Is prayer your go-
to? Is it the first thing you turn to when you are unsettled? Or does it feel
like another must-do on your never-ending to-do list? Knowing where to
start can be a challenge when you are faced with a giant-sized task. It helps
when someone else provides further context and spells out the next step
as you enter into the unknown.

## Focus

The book of Judges is positioned after the book of Joshua and is followed
by Ruth and 1 Samuel. In Joshua, we read about the Israelites experiencing
some victories over those who lived in the land that was promised to them
by God through His covenant with Abraham. Judges documents a time in

Israel's history where the twelve tribes began moving farther into their allotted territory but failed to take full possession of the land, enduring the consequences that accompanied their partial obedience instead of total obedience to God. God had warned them of the dangers of adopting the detestable practices of the surrounding nations, telling them it would lead to moral corruption and destruction (Deut. 7:16; 18:9–14).

### Strategically Positioned

God's people were instructed to live differently from the rest of the world. They were strategically positioned in a geographical location where international trading routes converged; other nations would take notice of the differences in their way of life and the ways of God. However, the Israelites did evil in His sight and did not carry out the clear instructions

**Trade Routes During the Reign of King Solomon**

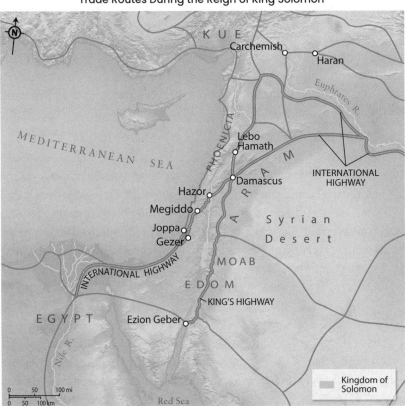

God had given them (Judg. 2:12). The surrounding nations oppressed them, and they cried out to God for deliverance. He responded by providing judges to lead them.

### SOS Prayers

My friend and Bible teacher Erica Wiggenhorn had a mentor who was nearing the end of his life. He had pastored people for decades upon decades and influenced Erica with his leadership and wisdom. She asked him to impart his best counsel to her as she continued to minister. This is what he said: "Little prayer, little power. Much prayer, much power."[1]

How often do we neglect the power of prayer and try to figure things out and complete tasks without seeking God's wisdom and asking for His help?

A few years ago, while I was driving to a prayer meeting, I was overwhelmed with all there was left to do for an upcoming event. Then God reminded me that much can be accomplished through prayer. Wherever I had gaps and lack, He could make a way. Even in areas where I had been faithless, He was, and is, faithful. I could try and muscle through on my limited strength, or I could turn to the limitless One who answers prayers, parts seas, multiplies loaves and fish, and still does miracles today.

If we want godly insight, relief from our burdens, and power beyond our own ability, prayer is the method God has graciously provided to us. It is how we directly communicate with Him.

> If we want godly insight, relief from our burdens, and power beyond our own ability, prayer is the method God has graciously provided to us. It is how we directly communicate with Him.

The other day, a friend said something like, "I don't pray as eloquently as other people do. My prayers are awkward and super simple." I assured her that fancy words don't impress God, and SOS prayers totally count.

"God, help!"

"God, please show me what to do!"

"God, I need You!"

What about you? What do you need help with? Are you feeling overwhelmed by all that is left undone? Do you feel alone in the decision-making process? Take a cue from the Israelites in Judges 1:1 and:

- Pray when you don't know the way.
- Pray when you feel alone.
- Pray when you are uncertain what's next.

After you pray, it's time to listen.

It can be tempting to make prayer a one-way conversation, to keep talking to God and pouring out our hurts, complaints, needs, and desires. We must remember to listen as well. While He wants us to pour out our hearts (and we should), it would be foolish to bypass the wisdom God is ready to impart. He speaks to us through His Spirit, Scripture, and godly counsel. Ask God to help you hear His voice. Ask Him if there is something impeding your ability to hear Him.

*Little prayer, little power.*
*Much prayer, much power.*

### Judges 1:1–2

After the death of Joshua, the Israelites inquired of the Lord. In the original language this word we translate as *inquired* means to "ask, beg, or borrow."[2] In the context of Judges 1:1, it means "to consult a deity." It was an SOS prayer.

"Who will be the first to fight for us against the Canaanites?" (Judg. 1:1). The Israelites' leader was dead, and they called out to God for direction. In verse 2, "The Lord answered, 'Judah is to go. I have handed the land over to him.'"

They received divine direction from God: the tribe of Judah was to go first. Not only did God answer their question but He also assured them of His promise—that He had handed the land over to Judah. In the next lesson, we will see if they obeyed or not.

Obedience can be an uncomfortable concept in an "anything goes" culture. It can sound harsh or outdated. But it is as necessary now as it has ever been.

Why might we resist when we hear the word *obey*? It might be because we have seen power abused, we want to call the shots, or we have felt let down by others or maybe even let down by God.

There is a famous line from C. S. Lewis's classic *The Horse and His Boy*, repeated several times throughout the story: "to hear is to obey."[3] This idea of hearing and obeying being one and the same principle dates back much further than Lewis, though. In ancient Jewish culture, these two words meant the same thing! The Hebrew word for "hear, listen to, and obey" is the word *shema* (pronounced shaw-mah').[4] This word

> is an excellent example of the difference between Hebrew, which stresses physical action[,] and Greek and Western culture that stresses mental activity. Listening, in our culture, is a mental activity, and hearing just means that our ears pick up sounds. But in Hebrew, the word *shema* describes hearing and also its effects—taking heed, being obedient, doing what is asked. Any parent who yells at their children, "Were you listening?" when they ignore a command to pick up their rooms understands that listening should result in action. In fact, almost every place we see the word "obey" in the Bible, it is translated from the word *shema*.[5]

Jewish people, then and now, call Deuteronomy 6:4–5 "the Shema." They pray these verses repeatedly: "Listen, Israel: The LORD our God, the LORD is one. Love the LORD your God with all your heart, with all your soul, and with all your strength."

This isn't just about reciting words. It's about living them out by loving the Lord your God with all your heart, soul, and strength. This love is all-encompassing, all in, holding nothing back. It's giving God access to every part of you, a complete surrender with a heart ready to listen and obey.

To hear is to obey. It is not only listening but doing.

Author Lois Tverberg says this well: "Hebrews understood that we have not truly put what we have heard into our hearts until it transforms our lives as well."[6] No wonder we are floundering. We have basically abandoned this concept and lifestyle of *shema*!

### Engage

1. Look up the following verses about prayer. Record what you learn.

   Psalm 66:17–20

   Psalm 116:1–2

   1 John 5:13–15

2. Look up the following verses about listening to God and God answering us. Record what you learn.

   Jeremiah 44:2–6

John 10:24–28

Revelation 3:19–22

3. Look up the following verses about obeying God. Record what you learn.

Matthew 7:24–27

John 15:9–10

James 1:22–25

## Reflect

Write out a prayer to God that includes a question. Listen for God's response. Obey what He says.

For example:

My prayer: *God, what should I do about that misunderstanding I had last week?*

His answer: *Let Me handle it. Learn from the situation but, in this instance, you don't need to say anything more.*

My response: *Obey God by trusting Him to handle this situation and not trying to fix it myself with many—or any—words.*

## Bonus

Judah was not the firstborn; he was the fourth son of Jacob and Leah. Jacob was Isaac's son and Abraham's grandson. Judah was chosen by God to be the tribe that Jesus came from, though he made some major mistakes in his life you can read about in Genesis 38. This is quite a scandalous story; record three main points from the passage:

Judah also made some good choices; read Genesis 37:26–28; 44:18–34. Record three main points from the passages:

Judah's father, Jacob, blessed him in Genesis 49:8–12. Record three of the main details of the blessing:

Genesis 49:10 contains foreshadowing of the coming Christ: "The scepter will not depart from Judah or the staff from between his feet until he whose right it is comes and the obedience of the peoples belongs to him."

Judah's story is about more than his sins and successes. God, in His sovereignty, mercy, and grace, chose the tribe of Judah for His special purposes. It wasn't earned; it was gifted.

Aren't we glad that God does not deal with us as our sins deserve? He restores and reinstates us because of His sovereignty, mercy, and grace and uses us for His purposes, pointing us and others to our desperate need for Jesus, the Lion of Judah.

## DECIDE

When you aren't sure what to do first,
decide to pray, listen, obey . . . and repeat.

# "God, What Do I Do When I Need Help?"

Judah said to his brother Simeon, "Come with me to my allotted territory, and let's fight against the Canaanites. I will also go with you to your allotted territory." So Simeon went with him.

JUDGES 1:3

## Read

JUDGES 1:3–11

Are you willing to help others but struggle when it comes to others helping you? Or do you readily accept help but struggle with an inclination to help others? Either way, I am sure each of us has room to grow in this area of helping and being helped. Today, we will look at two of the tribes of Israel and how they assisted one another with a giant-sized task.

## Focus

In Judges 1:2, the Israelites received their answer from the Lord: the tribe of Judah was to go first to fight against the Canaanites. God reminded them

He had handed the land over to Judah. In Judges 1:3, we observe that the tribe of Judah asked the tribe of Simeon to go with them to their allotted territory and fight against the Canaanites together. Judah gave his word that he would also go with Simeon to his allotted territory.

### Being With and For

Circle the following phrases in Judges 1:3 at the top of this lesson:

- with me
- let us
- with you
- with him

There is comfort in knowing we are not alone, especially when we are entering a battle of some kind.

The tribe of Judah was far from perfect, yet they were blessed by God and chosen to be the family line from which Jesus, the Great Deliverer, would come (Gen. 49:8–12; Ps. 78:67–68; Rev. 5:5).

Matthew Henry's commentary describes the difference in size between the two tribes of Israel:

> Judah was the most considerable of all the tribes, and Simeon the least; yet Judah begs Simeon's friendship, and prays for aid from him. It becomes Israelites to help one another against Canaanites; and all Christians, even those of different tribes, should strengthen one another. Those who thus help one another in love, have reason to hope that God will graciously help both.[1]

God was *with* Judah. And Judah going first was a picture of the Lord going before us in battle. Judah and Simeon supporting one another in battle is a powerful visual of being *with* and *for* one another, unified around God's instructions.

It's fascinating to observe the collaboration of these two tribes. They were vastly different in size and strength, yet they served one another instead of being intimidated by or discounting the other. They were unified in purpose. Let Judah and Simeon in Judges 1 serve as an example of what it looks like to go *with* someone, to be *for* them, even when drastic differences are present.

### Stronger Together

At a community prayer gathering, an intercessor named Lori said, "There is a greater strength present when the individual churches come together in unity." We can accomplish things on our own and we each have strength from the Lord, but when we link arms with other believers and follow God's marching orders, we are unstoppable. We have a greater strength.

**It can be easier to follow through in obeying the Lord when we have companionship and accountability along the way.**

Whether we have much or little, God instructs us to faithfully steward what we have been entrusted with. The power to complete our sacred assignments comes from God, and the results are up to Him, yet we have an active role to play in His kingdom. Maybe that is in prayer, or giving, or labor, or sacrifice, or staying quiet when we'd rather speak, or speaking up and standing up to injustice, or engaging in difficult conversations, or walking through the doors He has opened even when we are scared, or a myriad of other things. Our part is to obey and lean into His wisdom and strength as we do.

Are you vigorously applying yourself in service to God?

Are you worn out or poured out for God?

There is a difference. Wearing yourself out is often based on striving and trying to prove yourself, but pouring yourself out is operating from the overflow, in obedience and gratitude.

It can be easier to follow through in obeying the Lord when we have companionship and accountability along the way.

## Engage

1. Summarize what Judah and Simeon were able to accomplish together, with the Lord's help (Judg. 1:4–5).

2. Look up the following Scriptures and write them out below. Pay attention to what you learn: about God, about obeying Him, and about being in community with others. Then, answer the questions based on what you read in Judges and in the given passage.

   **Exodus 14:13–14.** Prior to the time of Judges, Moses gave these instructions to the Israelites. What does it look like to let the Lord fight for you? What is His part and what is your part in the battles you face?

   **Nehemiah 4:14.** Although this verse refers to another time in Israel's history, the principle of fighting for, not against, your countrymen and family applies to this passage in Judges. How does the concept of being united in purpose help Judah and Simeon carry out God's instructions in Judges 1:2?

**Romans 12:16.** How might this verse apply to the partnership between Judah and Simeon?

### The Rest of the Story

Judges 1:4–11 is graphic. Judah and Simeon cut off their enemies' thumbs and toes; they set cities on fire. Rather than getting hung up on the brutality, remember the broader point is they asked God for insight, He answered them, and they obeyed Him. The tribes of Judah and Simeon worked together to accomplish His purposes even when the stakes were high and the task looked impossible. There is more to the story here: past injustices, grievous sins, idol worship. God's people had specific instructions to fight against that which opposed God and His ways, not for violence's sake but because they had a greater need for total deliverance from the sin that so easily entangled them and drew them away from God (Heb. 12:10–13).

God was jealous for His people. He did not want anything to stand between them and Him. He was *with* them and *for* them. He was and is Emmanuel, God with us.

### God with Us

Your heavenly Father is a Promise Keeper. He has not left you alone. His availability to you is unmatched. He isn't too busy for you. He does not dismiss you. He doesn't grow tired of you. God cares for you more than you can imagine. His presence goes before you and is with you, and He will give you rest (Exod. 33:12–17).

Not only is God with us but He calls us to do the same for our brothers and sisters in Christ. It is a beautiful thing to be in community with one another, to do life together, to hang in there when times are difficult and uncertain. It is not easy, but it is possible through the guidance and strength He supplies.

Recently I was asked to lead worship for an upcoming ladies' event. I could have done it myself, but I knew that if I invited my friend Cherri, we'd be able to combine our God-given strengths and have greater impact together. Either one of us could have led effectively in this regard, yet we were willing to lay aside our pride and individual giftedness in order to collaborate for the kingdom. It may have been simpler for us to lead alone, but we saw the value of putting in more work in order to maximize the result and encourage each other in the process.

## Reflect

1. In what ways are you faithfully stewarding the people and tasks God has assigned to you?

2. In what ways are you fighting against your brothers and sisters in Christ? Why do you think that is?

3. What does it look like to fight *for* your brothers and sisters? Give a specific example from your own life or one you have observed in others.

4. Are you letting intimidation stop you from cooperation? Why or why not?

5. In what ways are you discounting what others bring to the table?

**Bonus**

Record what you learn about being a faithful steward from Matthew 25:14–30; Luke 16:10–12; and 1 Corinthians 4:1–2. How will this impact your daily decisions?

If you are curious why Simeon was so much smaller of a tribe than Judah, find the answer in Genesis 34:24–30; Genesis 49:1–2, 5–12; and 1 Chronicles 4:24–27. Record your findings below, as well as your reaction to what you discovered.

Read Romans 12:9–21 to glean deeper insight into what it means to obey God by being *for* other people. Write out one of the verses from this passage that convicted you the most. How can you begin implementing it with God's help?

## DECIDE

When you need help, decide to obey God by being *with* and *for* one another, according to His example and His instructions.

# "God, What Do I Do with What You've Given Me?"

The LORD was with Judah and enabled them to take possession of the hill country, but they could not drive out the people
who were living in the plain because those people had iron
chariots.

JUDGES 1:19

## Read

JUDGES 1:12–20

You have been given more than you may realize—promises, position, possessions, and people. What will you do with what God has entrusted to
you? Whether much or little in the world's eyes, you have been given time,
talents, and treasures to faithfully offer during your lifetime. Will you withhold what you have been gifted or seek to honor God generously?

## Focus

According to Genesis 17:8, it was God who gave the Israelites the land of Canaan as their allotted territory—their permanent possession, through His permanent covenant with Abraham. God also revealed Himself to Abraham's son Isaac, reminding him of all He had promised his father (26:1–6). To recap from the introductory lesson, God promised, through His covenant with Abraham, the following:

- God would be with Abraham and bless him and give the Promised Land to his people.
- Abraham's offspring would be as numerous as the stars in the sky.
- All the nations of the earth would be blessed through Abraham's descendants.

Genesis 26:5 gives us the reason for this: "because Abraham listened to me and kept my mandate, my commands, my statutes, and my instructions." God also revealed Himself to Jacob, Isaac's son (28:10–15). God reminded Jacob of all that had been promised. I find great comfort in the assuring words God gave Jacob in verse 15: "Look, I am with you and will watch over you wherever you go. I will bring you back to this land, for I will not leave you until I have done what I have promised you." It is worth noting that these three men, Abraham, Isaac, and Jacob, made some big mistakes, yet God chose them and used them to establish a new nation that was called to be set apart for Him and point the world to Him. Jacob was later named Israel, and his sons became the twelve tribes of the nation of Israel.

### *Allotted Territory*

The beginning of Judges 1:3 focuses on two of the tribes of Israel, Judah and Simeon, who were descendants of Jacob's sons. Judah asked Simeon to come with him to his *allotted territory*, and then he told Simeon that he would also go with him to his *allotted territory*.

The map below outlines the allotted territory of the tribes of Israel.

Image provided by Luke Taylor, 2BeLikeChrist.com; reprinted by permission.

Mediterranean
Sea

Tyre

Damascus •

▲ Mt. Hermon

Dan •

**NAPHTALI**

Hazor •

**ASHER**

Merom •

**EAST MANASSEH**

Sea of Galilee

**ZEBULUN**

Kishon River

**ISSACHAR**

▲ ← Mt. Tabor

Jordan River

Jezreel •

▲ ← Mt. Gilboa

**Gilead**

**WEST
MANASSEH**

• Abel-meholah

Thebez •

Zaphon •

Shechem •

Succoth •

• Mahanaim

Mt. Gerizim ▲

• Penuel

Shiloh •

**GAD**

**Ammon**

**EPHRAIM**

Bethel (Luz) •

Gilgal •

**BENJAMIN**

Gibeah •

Jericho

**DAN**

• Jerusalem

• Ekron

Ashdod

Timnah •

Zorah •

Gath •

↑

Ashkelon

Lehi

**REUBEN**

Eglon •

• Hebron

Dead
Sea

Gaza •

**JUDAH**

• Aroer

• Bethel

Moab

• Beersheba

**SIMEON**

**Edom**

We each have allotted territory from God to enter, possess, and faithfully steward.

Another way we can define our allotted territory is to think about the people, position, and place we have been entrusted with during our time here on earth. For example: I have been entrusted with my husband and five children (my people), as well as a ministry to inspire others to walk in their God-given purpose. I am a wife and mom, and the roles of teacher, worship leader, author, speaker, and podcast host are the means through which I currently minister (my position). I live in the middle of Michigan on four acres, and I work and serve at a local church (my place).

> We each have allotted territory from God to enter, possess, and faithfully steward.

Don't discount your allotted territory. It might be vast or tiny or somewhere in between. The size and scope are not what matters. It is what you do with what you have been given that matters.

What **people** have you been entrusted with?

What **position** have you been entrusted with?

What **place** have you been entrusted with?

### Courageous Caleb

In Judges 1:12–20, we meet Caleb. Born into slavery, Caleb experienced the exodus as well as the wilderness years. Caleb's character was forged through four decades of slavery followed by four decades in the desert. What could have made him bitter made him faithful. Instead of allowing seeds of resentment to be planted, Caleb had faith that grew strong roots amid adversity.

Caleb was forty years old when Moses sent him and eleven other spies to scout out the Promised Land and report back what they found. Caleb and Joshua were the only ones who brought back a favorable report (Num. 13).

## Engage

1. Read Moses's and God's exchange about the wandering Israelites in Numbers 14:19–24 and write down a few things you learn about Caleb's character and God's promise to him.

2. In Joshua 14:6–9, we read more about Caleb. Record the phrases in verses 8 and 9 that describe the way in which Caleb followed God.

It is my prayer that you and I, like Caleb, would follow the Lord our God completely. Even in our old age, may we be able to echo Caleb's words: "I am still as strong today as I was the day Moses sent me out. My strength for battle and for daily tasks is now as it was then" (Josh. 14:11).

The hill country of Hebron was given to Caleb (14:4–14; 15:13–19). It appears that some of this account in Judges is a recap of what was written in Joshua 15. The Anakim lived in this region of the Promised Land, and because it contained large fortified cities, a battle was needed in order to drive the Anakim out.

Has God ever promised you something, but in order to enter and possess that promise, a battle of sorts was required? Why do you think that is?

What if the reason is to strengthen and prepare you to handle the challenges, blessings, and responsibility of the increased territory God is entrusting to you—whether that means more people in your life, a different position of influence, or a shift in your location? Will you believe God's promise and act on that promise? Will you resist trying to make it happen on your own strength and rely on God's power, following His directives when the time is right? Caleb was eighty-five when the promise he had been given came to fruition, and to enjoy that promise, he had an active part to play.

In Judges, we read that Caleb said he would give his daughter, Achsah, in marriage to whoever captured a portion of his land. He demonstrates the wisdom of delegation here. Othniel, the son of Caleb's younger brother Kenaz, captured it and married Achsah. In Judges 3 we learn that Othniel is the first judge God raises up (we will learn more about him in Week 3).

### A Blessing Bestowed

In Judges 1:14–15, we read that Achsah persuaded her husband, Othniel, to ask her father, Caleb, for a field. She wanted a blessing. She boldly asked him for more territory in her allotment. Her father had already given her land in the desert, Negev, but she wanted a spring too. So, Caleb gave her the upper and lower springs.

The question Caleb asked his daughter in verse 14, "What do you want?," reminds me of the question God asked Solomon in 2 Chronicles 1:7, "Ask. What should I give you?" In verse 10, Solomon answered, "Now grant me wisdom and knowledge so that I may lead these people, for who can judge this great people of yours?" Solomon said this during the time of the kings in Israel, which came after the time of the judges. His answer reveals that judging the people of Israel was a weighty task that required great wisdom, beyond his natural ability. As we learn more about the first judges in upcoming lessons, we will find this to be true. Supernatural insight is needed to navigate uncertain times—then and now.

### The Inhabitants of Mountains and Valleys

In Judges 1:16, we read about the descendants of Moses's father-in-law, Jethro the Kenite. These people had gone up to live among the people in the wilderness of Judah, which was in the Negev of Arad. I had the privilege of visiting Tel Arad on my trip to Israel in June 2018. It was amazing to walk among the remains of this ancient site, which dates to the tenth century. According to the Israel Nature and Parks Authority, "Tel Arad is one of the most important archaeological sites in Israel, on which were found the remains of a fortified Canaanite City and fortresses from the time of the Kings of Judah."[1]

Keep the Kenites in mind as you study. They will come into play later, in a major way!

Judges 1:17–19 describes more about the conquests of Judah and Simeon. Our focus verse for this lesson is verse 19. Let's read it again: "The LORD was with Judah and enabled them to take possession of the hill country, but they could not drive out the people who were living in the plain because those people had iron chariots."

On one hand this is a comforting verse, reinforcing what we learned in the previous lesson: the Lord was *with* the tribe of Judah. However, the latter part of this verse is troubling. Why do you think they couldn't drive out the inhabitants of the valley? Was God not strong enough, was their faith not big enough, or was it something else?

Verse 19 says they could not drive out the inhabitants. It does not say God could not drive them out. It seems Judah operated in the strength God provided—until they were faced with the impossible obstacle of iron chariots.

### Battle Plans

We are going to take a brief departure from Judges and look at a handful of verses throughout Scripture to help us understand God's instruction for His people during battle. Keep Judges 1:19 in mind as you engage with the following verses.

1. In Deuteronomy 20:1–4, God gave His people laws concerning warfare. He even addressed the intimidating iron chariots. Record the four "do nots" given to the people when they engaged in battle.

Do not:

Do not:

Do not:

Do not:

2. Write out Deuteronomy 20:4 below. How is this verse similar to Judges 1:19?

3. Read Psalm 33:16–22. According to these verses, we are to:

- Fear God.
- Depend on His faithful love to rescue us from death and keep us alive in famine.
- Wait for the Lord.
- Rejoice in Him.
- Trust in His holy name.
- Put our hope in God.

Circle one of these instructions. What is one specific way you can obey that instruction today?

4. Turn what you learned into a prayer. In other words, pray Scripture back to God. You can't go wrong in doing that. Here's an example to get you started, from Psalm 33:16–22:

*Dear God, thank You that I can put my hope in You, even when I face my own version of iron chariots. Horses, armies, and governmental leaders are not what save us. I want to trust in You more—not in my own strength or wisdom but Yours. May Your faithful love rest on me, Lord, for I put my hope in You. Amen.*

Your turn: *Dear God . . .*

### Iron Chariots

Let's evaluate the iron chariots from two different angles. First, let's look at the Canaanites' perspective. They worshiped other gods and did not believe in the One True God. They demonstrated technological advancement by defending themselves with iron chariots. The chariots weren't bad in and of themselves, but their trust in them was misguided and shortsighted.

When we face valleys—low times—in our lives, we can create our own version of "iron chariots" to defend our weak areas. Valley times are vulnerable times, and it makes sense to want to protect ourselves against further attack. But what if the "iron chariots" we construct to defend ourselves end up being an obstruction to experiencing complete restoration? What if instead of depending on ourselves to keep the enemy at bay, we leaned in to the One who knows exactly how to expose, defeat, and eradicate anything between us and our Great Deliverer, and between us and living in the Promised Land?

Now let's look at these iron chariots from the perspective of the tribes of Judah and Simeon. When faced with the reality that they were going to fight people with superior armaments, they did not complete their directive to fully possess the land. It appears their faith waned when the odds—as they saw them with their natural eyes—were stacked against them.

> What if the "iron chariots" we construct to defend ourselves end up being an obstruction to experiencing complete restoration?

God promised to give Judah success, yet in the presence of the enemy's iron chariots, Judah's courage melted into cowardice. The tribe of Judah was fighting well, but when faced with these intimidating weapons, they hightailed it out of battle. Not only did they fail to complete their mission but their disobedience impacted the other tribes.

As we learned in the introductory lesson, it is imperative to remember what God has done in the past because it provides wisdom as to how we are to proceed, and it fortifies our faith going forward. Not that long before the time of the judges, God effectively dealt with the threat of chariots. How quickly the Israelites had forgotten God's complete ability to rescue them.

When God delivered His people from slavery in Egypt, the Israelites were soon pursued by Pharaoh and his troops, including "six hundred of the best chariots and all the rest of the chariots of Egypt, with officers in each one" (Exod. 14:7). The Egyptians chased after the Israelites and caught up with them, and the Israelites cried out to the Lord for help. They told Moses that it would have been better for them to remain in Egypt as slaves than to die in the wilderness (vv. 11–12). It was a terrifying situation, but God had an unexpected plan to protect His people. Moses reassured them, "Don't be afraid. Stand firm and see the LORD's salvation that he will accomplish for you today; for the Egyptians you see today, you will never see again. The LORD will fight for you, and you must be quiet" (vv. 13–14).

God proceeded to protect His people by placing a pillar of cloud between the Egyptian and Israelite forces (vv. 19–20). He parted the Red Sea so His people could escape on dry ground.

> Then the LORD said to Moses, "Stretch out your hand over the sea so that the water may come back on the Egyptians, on their chariots and horsemen." So Moses stretched out his hand over the sea, and at daybreak the sea returned to its normal depth. While the Egyptians were trying to escape from it, the LORD threw them into the sea. The water came back and covered the chariots and horsemen, plus the entire army of Pharaoh that had gone after them into the sea. Not even one of them survived. (vv. 26–28)

This is how God dealt with the threat of chariots in the past. The enemy and the weapons that were positioned to take out His children were no match for the Lord.

Psalm 68:17 states that God's chariots are tens of thousands—*thousands and thousands*. He is the God of angel armies. That's who our God is! Iron chariots have nothing on Him. God can deliver vulnerable people from the pursuit of a well-trained army (Exod. 14:5–28) and defeat giants with a single stone (1 Sam. 17:48–51). He can deliver His people from fiery furnaces (Dan. 3:8–25), the mouths of lions (6:16–24), and the clutches of a crazed king (Ps. 18). He can defend us and deliver us when we see no way out.

*O God, may we not stop short of fully obeying You, even when we are intimidated by the enemy. Help us stand our ground, knowing that You are greater than anything we face. May we be found faithful to finish the work You have entrusted us to do. In the mighty name of Jesus, Amen.*

## Reflect

1. What iron chariots are you coming up against in your allotted territory? In other words, what obstacles are present regarding your people, your position, your place? These obstacles might be self-erected, or they might be outside of your control.

2. Are there iron chariots you are trusting in more than God? *For example: your bank account, intelligence, talents, physical strength, friends, or significant other.*

3. What is hindering your ability to fully possess what's rightfully yours as a child of God? Be honest with the Lord and yourself, and maybe also a trusted friend, as you ponder this question.

## Bonus

Read Psalm 33 in its entirety. It provides clarity on God's capabilities and further direction for God's people. What is a key word, a phrase, and a sentence from this psalm that stand out to you? Record those below.

Word:

Phrase:

Sentence:

## DECIDE

When you aren't sure what to do with what you've been given, decide to obey the Lord by faithfully stewarding the people, position, and place He has entrusted to you.

# "God, What Do I Do When You Speak to Me?"

At the same time the Benjaminites did not drive out the Jebusites who were living in Jerusalem. The Jebusites have lived among the Benjaminites in Jerusalem to this day.

JUDGES 1:21

### Read

JUDGES 1:21–26

Have you ever tried to justify your way out of obedience to God? I have.

Just a few days ago, it came to my attention that I only had a few hours left to declare my intent to run for our local school board. For a few brief moments, I almost delayed my obedience to follow through on this clear directive from the Lord. My thought process went something like this: *I am unclear on all the steps, so maybe I could wait until next year, then I will do it.* Part of the temptation to delay my obedience was all the time, resources, and intensity this decision to run for office would mean for me and my family.

But with God's direction and the support of others, I was able to get my paperwork done in time. I felt nervous, excited, and overwhelmed. Tears welled up in response to the heaviness and the honor of this endeavor. The results are up to God. My role is to obey His voice and follow His lead—even when it is uncomfortable, inconvenient, or difficult.

## Focus

When faced with the iron chariots, the tribes of Judah and Simeon stopped short in carrying out God's divine direction. They retreated when faced with intimidating opposition. They did not inquire of the Lord to see how to address the iron chariot issue. They did not obey Him. They did not fully possess the place God had promised them. And their example set a precedence of partial obedience to the other tribes.

### The Consequences of Disobedience

In Judges 1:21 we read about what the Benjaminites were doing at this time. They did not drive out the Jebusites who were living in Jerusalem. And because of this, the Jebusites lived among them "to this day." The Jebusites were descendants of Canaan, the fourth son of Ham. Ham was one of Noah's sons (Gen. 10:1, 6, 15–16). In Deuteronomy 20:16–18, God commanded the Israelites to completely destroy six people groups, including the Jebusites. He gave the reason for this in verse 18: "so that they won't teach you to do all the detestable acts they do for their gods, and you sin against the LORD your God."

Again, we see a pattern of disobedience among God's people. Why? Were they afraid, lazy, complacent, or rebellious? Their success was ensured, if they would just do their part. Why didn't they fully follow the instructions God gave them?

Why don't *we* fully obey Him?

Did they—do we—not believe what He says is true?

Are we dealing with a spirit of unbelief here?

Our obedience, or lack thereof, does not only affect us but impacts those around us, including future generations.

> Our obedience, or lack thereof, does not only affect us but impacts those around us, including future generations.

We are still dealing with the consequences from Adam and Eve sinning against God (Gen. 3) and the animosity in the Middle East between the descendants of Isaac and Ishmael due to Abraham and Sarah taking matters into their own hands instead of waiting on God's timing to fulfill His promise of giving them a son, even in their old age (Gen. 16).

### The Blessing of Obedience

God sent Jesus to redeem us from eternal separation from Him, and if we believe He is the Savior and accept Him as our Lord, He gives us mercy, forgiveness, and grace. That is amazing and undeserved! Yet we can still experience natural consequences for our sin. This is not because God is unloving; in fact, it is quite the opposite. When we feel the weight of our poor choices, it motivates us to repent and change. The struggle refines and matures us.

We also experience blessings in our lives as a result of our obedience, and sometimes as a result of the obedience of others.

Through Jesus we can receive the blessing of the forgiveness of our sins and eternal life with Him instead of the grave consequence of carrying the guilt of our sins: eternal separation from Him.

## Engage

Read Romans 5:12–21 and record the differences between Adam and Jesus below.

| Adam | Jesus |
| --- | --- |
|  |  |

Jesus knew the Father's plan and obediently followed it: to save us from our helpless state. He took on our consequences so we could receive salvation. If Jesus had only partially obeyed, salvation would not be possible for us.

Although Jesus primarily ministered on earth to the descendants of Abraham, He demonstrated to them that all peoples are worthy of His love, time, and deliverance.

### The Ripple Effect

While in Israel, I visited the Decapolis region, which is east and southeast of the Sea of Galilee. This is where the demon-possessed man was delivered by Jesus and the demons were cast into the herd of pigs that jumped off a cliff and drowned (Mark 5:1–20).

After his healing, Jesus told this man he couldn't come with Him. He instructed him to stay in the area he lived in and tell his people the great things Jesus had done for him, the mercy he had been shown. Mark 5:20 reveals that this man obeyed. And not just partially.

Don't underestimate the power of one person's obedience and the power of a changed life by Christ.

Later on, Jesus returned to this region (6:53–56). It is clear that the once demon-possessed man had obeyed His instructions, because many, many people ran to Jesus for healing. This man hadn't been given a pamphlet about "How to Give Your Testimony in Three Easy Steps." He simply obeyed Jesus, telling those around him about what Jesus had done for him. His obedience had a ripple effect, blessing his community and coming generations, including us.

> Don't underestimate the power of one person's obedience and the power of a changed life by Christ.

Jesus's no ushered in a greater yes!

Jesus has laid out clear instructions in His Word for how we are to live. When we are not sure what we are to do next for a job, in a relationship, or about a battle in our lives, we can run to Jesus and fully follow the divine directives He has already given us.

Today, for me, obedience looks like designing election materials for my school board race.

Our obedience always has a ripple effect, influencing our family line and our community for good—and maybe even an entire region of people who would not have heard about Jesus otherwise.

### To This Day

Before we wrap up this lesson, reread Judges 1:22–26. Here we see the house of Joseph attacking Bethel. The Lord was *with* them. They sent out spies into Bethel, and they soon saw a man coming out of the town. The spies asked this man to show them how to get into the town and gave their word that they would show this man from Bethel kindness if he would help them. The meaning of "kindness" here, in the original language, is astounding. The word is *chesed*, and it is the common word for God's loyal, covenant-based love.[1] An all-in, with-you-till-the-end kind of love.

This man showed the spies the way into Bethel, and when the Israelites overtook the town, they released him and his entire family and delivered them from harm. This man's decision not only affected himself but also his whole family.

The last phrase in Judges 1:21 is "to this day." The tribe of Benjamin disobeyed God's command to fully enter into the land He gave them, and they weren't just impacted then but *to this day*. Their disobedience impacted coming generations.

Judges 1:26 reveals the actions of this man from Bethel, after he and his entire family were released: "Then the man went to the land of the Hittites, built a town, and named it Luz. That is its name still today." This man helped God's people, and he and his family were spared. His cooperation impacted coming generations.

We see with the tribe of Benjamin that disobedience is a serious matter. It can negatively affect us for a long time. We see with the demon-possessed man that obedience is a serious matter. It can positively alter the trajectory of a multitude of people.

What if Jesus's instructions to this man are the same to us? "Go home to your own people, and report to them how much the Lord has done for you and how he has had mercy on you" (Mark 5:19).

Jesus's *chesed*—His loyal, covenant-based love—still impacts us to this day. His obedience has a ripple effect, delivering all those who run to Him from sin and death and to salvation.

**Reflect**

1. Think about someone you know who made a courageous choice to obey God, even in the face of many obstacles. Consider sharing this example below and/or with others.

2. What is one courageous decision you need to make today?

3. How will the decisions you make today not only bless your people now but also bless your future descendants?

**Bonus**

The book of Ruth takes place in the time of the judges. Read Ruth 4:9–22 to see *chesed* (God's loyal, covenant-based love) on display as Boaz redeems the widow Ruth and the tribe of Judah continues through their union, leading toward King David and, ultimately, the Messiah, the King of kings, sent to redeem us all.

## DECIDE

When God speaks to you, decide to obey
God completely, not halfway.

# "God, What Do I Do When I've Failed?"

When Israel became stronger, they made the Canaanites
serve as forced labor but never drove them out completely.

JUDGES 1:28

**Read**

JUDGES 1:27–36

Have you failed at something lately? Failing is not my favorite. I like to meet or exceed expectations—except when it comes to pesky, annoying things that are a nuisance to tackle. I tend to avoid those kinds of tasks or only partially address them.

In the summer, my family often battles with small ants in our house. Gross, I know. They are especially drawn to honey and anything sweet. My husband has concocted a homemade spray to wipe them out. He has given us clear instructions on how to take care of the pests, either with a foot stomp or the spray. I must admit, I sometimes just brush an ant out of my sight instead of taking care of business. But ignoring these intruders in my home does not make them go away.

On a bigger scale, there are lies and evil influences that intrude upon our homes on a regular basis. What will our approach be? Will we brush them off and pretend they don't exist, or will we assertively attack the lies with the truth and annihilate that which threatens to invade what we have been entrusted with?

Could it be that tiny untruths are beginning to cross the boundary lines, taking up residence in the real estate of your mind? Left unaddressed, these lies can begin to take over until your home becomes a place you no longer recognize. Thankfully, God provides the wisdom and strength you need to overcome.

## Focus

Sometimes obedience is exhausting. It can feel easier to cut corners instead of completing the directive with which we've been charged. Maybe we need to reframe our view of obedience. Instead of it being a pressure to perform, what if we viewed it as a matter of being set free? Of abundance instead of lack? Or life instead of death?

Today's passage does not mince words. It calls out the failure of some of the tribes of Israel to fully drive out the surrounding nations. They cut corners and reaped the consequences. It is a stark reminder of humanity's desperate need for a Savior. When we're weak, He is strong. When we fail, He succeeds. When we confess our sin, He forgives.

Jesus's obedience saved lives. In Him we are truly forgiven and freed, released from the clutches of captivity.

## Engage

When you study the Bible, it is important to pay attention to key repeated words or phrases. Judges 1:27–36 includes many place names you may find hard to pronounce. But stay focused on these key words/phrases:

- Failed (to drive out)
- Determined (to stay)
- Forced labor
- Living among them (or living in the land)

Let's go through these one by one, answering the questions that follow.

**Failure.** *Failure* is a strong word. I don't think any of us would want our failures published for all to see. Yet reflecting on our failures and/or the failures of others can serve as an effective teaching tool. Not so we can judge or condemn but so we can learn and grow. We have an opportunity to do things differently. His mercies are new every morning. Can I get an AMEN?

1. Who failed to obey God's instructions to fully possess the land?

   - Manasseh

   - E

   - Z

   - A

   - N

   - Danites

**Determined.** Other words for *determined* are *resolved* or *persisted*. The Canaanites *persisted* in dwelling there. Apparently, they were more determined to stay put than God's people were to obey Him.

**Forced labor.** The Israelites were well acquainted with forced labor. When they were in Egypt, they were subject to Pharaoh's oppressive rule for centuries. They cried out to God for deliverance from their bondage. As recorded in Judges 1:28, 30, 33, and 35, the Canaanites were made to serve the Israelites with forced labor. They were supposed to be driven out completely, but because the Israelites did not completely obey God, the Canaanites lived among them.

> The Canaanites were to be eradicated, not enslaved. The Israelites were to be set apart, not enmeshed with sin.

The Canaanites were to be eradicated, not enslaved. The Israelites were to be set apart, not enmeshed with sin.

Time and time again, God was gracious to His wayward people. He wanted—and still wants—better for them, and for us.

**Living among them (or living in the land).** Today's passage lists many of those whom the Israelites lived among. Where the Israelites had cut corners, they now had to deal with the reality and inconvenience of their disobedience. The conflict they initially avoided only intensified over time.

1. Read Deuteronomy 20:16–18 to see what God's instructions were to His people regarding those who were living in the land of Canaan.

2. In verse 18, God gives the reason why His people were to battle in this way. What did He say would happen if they did not obey what He had instructed? (Hint: how would they be negatively influenced?)

3. Read Galatians 5:7–10 and describe how it expounds on this idea of being drawn away from obedience.

In other words, a little sin, a little disobedience, a little dishonesty can work its way into our lives and negatively impact us in a big way—leading us away from sound decisions and leading us toward bondage instead of freedom. God loved His people and knew what was best for them; therefore, He instructed them so that it would go well for them. His commands of obedience have always been given out of His fierce love for us.

Ultimately, God sent Jesus to live among His people so He could, once and for all, provide deliverance from sin—theirs and ours. His influence can turn us from disobedience and toward obedience if we willingly grow in our trust of Him and cooperate with Him, not as forced laborers but as willing children who want to honor their Good Father.

Not sure what to do?

Not sure which way to go?

You can't go wrong by obeying God.

The bottom line is this: God's instructions in the Bible are saturated with wisdom and rooted in His rich love for you. He is trustworthy.

> God's instructions in the Bible are saturated with wisdom and rooted in His rich love for you. He is trustworthy.

Psalm 25:8–13 contains powerful truths that summarize what we have learned. Read through these verses slowly. Ponder the clear direction they provide for daily living.

> The LORD is good and upright;
> therefore he shows sinners the way.
> He leads the humble in what is right
> and teaches them his way.
> All the LORD's ways show faithful love and truth
> to those who keep his covenant and decrees.
> LORD, for the sake of your name,
> forgive my iniquity, for it is immense.
>
> Who is this person who fears the LORD?
> He will show him the way he should choose.
> He will live a good life,
> and his descendants will inherit the land.

## Reflect

As we end this lesson, read through the **OBEY** acronym.

**O** pportunities to trust God's character are gifts to grow you.

**B** lessings await those who follow God's commands.

**E** xercising your faith strengthens your faith.

**Y** ielding your will to God's leadership is wise.

> Visit KatieMReid.com/Judges to access a beautiful printable of this acronym to remind you of the benefits of obedience.

1. Which statement sticks out to you the most from the OBEY acronym and why?

2. Have you ever been undeterred in your determination to stay put, even when God was clearly telling you to move? What were the circumstances surrounding this determination?

3. Think of an example from your own life, the life of someone you know, or Scripture that demonstrates undeterred determination in the face of opposition, for good. Jot down a few sentences about it.

4. Is there an area in your life where God is asking you to move, either toward something or away from something, or maybe actually to move from one location to another? What is holding you back from obeying Him?

5. Write out a prayer asking for God's help to fully obey Him. He is ready and willing to help you move—step by step. Lean in to His strength and guidance.

*Dear God . . .*

## Bonus

Read Deuteronomy 30 for insight into what God promised those who obeyed Him.

### DECIDE

When you have failed, decide to obey and live in freedom instead of bondage.

*Dear Jesus,*

*Forgive me for not completely obeying You. I need Your help to trust You more. Help me not to view Your commands as prohibitive but as protective, not as limitations but as liberty, and not as restrictions but as wisdom. You do not want me to be bound by the chains of bitterness, shame, rebellion, revenge, fear, unforgiveness, or any other sins. In many ways I have called the shots and been wise in my own eyes. But You see it all. You know it all. Lead me back to You. It is time for me to put the past behind me, along with my old ways of thinking. Renew my mind according to Your never-changing truth (Rom. 12:1–2). May what I think about, say, and do honor You (Phil. 4:8).*

*Show me the areas in which I am still living as a slave instead of a blood-bought, Spirit-filled, dearly loved child of God. You died so I could be free indeed. I want to run in the path of Your commandments, for You have set my heart free (Ps. 119:32). Show me, step by step, how to honor You in my decisions, for that is the right thing to do, and bless-ing awaits those who choose to follow Your instructions. You lead me in love. Even when the water is deep, the mountain is steep, the valley is lonely . . . You are there. You are well acquainted with suffering and grief. You understand my pain. You know how to overcome temptation, and You are interceding for me right now—praying according to what is best.*

*I want to live in a way that brings glory to You, even when I feel scared, unsure, or frustrated. Thank You that You are greater than any iron chariot I face. You promise I have a delightful inheritance in You (Eph. 1:3, 11–14). I don't want to miss out on all of who You are and all You have for me. Teach me how to obey You, and may I get better at it day by day. In Jesus's name, Amen.*

## WEEK 1 WRAP-UP

*This week, I decide to obey God's commands completely, not partially.*

Answer the following questions to help summarize what you learned during this week of study. If possible, use biblical references to back up your responses.

1. Judges 1:19 and Judges 1:22 talk about the Lord being

   _____ the tribe of Judah and _____ the house of

   Joseph. How has God been *with* you this week?

2. What is one of the commands God gave His people regarding the allotted territory He entrusted to them?

3. How does the Bible define obedience, based on the Scriptures you read this week?

4. Read 2 John 1:4–6. What does it look like to love God, according to verse 6?

5. Based on what you discovered in Lessons 1–5, how can the decision to obey help you make wise decisions in uncertain times?

# THE DECISION TO BE RESPONSIBLE

## JUDGES 2

God's people only partially obeyed His command to fully possess the Promised Land. As we dig into Judges 2 this week, we will focus on the consequences of the Israelites' disobedience and God's mercy in raising up judges to protect them from their enemies (military protection) and from the influence of their enemies (moral protection). We will discover that the decision to be responsible to God for our actions can fortify our faith and positively influence those around us, especially in trying times.

**KEY VERSE: JUDGES 2:22**

I did this to test Israel and to see whether or not they would keep the LORD's way by walking in it, as their ancestors had.

# "God, What Do I Do When I'm Trapped by Sin?"

You are not to make a covenant with the inhabitants of this land. You are to tear down their altars. But you have not obeyed me. What have you done?

JUDGES 2:2

## Read

JUDGES 2:1–5

In what ways have you felt trapped by sin? Like you couldn't shake it, even though you knew it was destructive? Maybe it's an addiction or overspending, maybe it's gossip or cutting words, maybe it's a secret sin or a blatant lie. Aren't you relieved that God provides a way of escape for us when we are stuck? He is stronger than any hang-up we have, and He is able to restore us from the inside out. The first step is admitting what we are struggling with and asking for His help. "SOS, God! I can't do this without Your intervention."

## Focus

After Adam and Eve disobeyed God and ate from the tree of the knowledge of good and evil in the garden of Eden, they did not take responsibility for their actions (Gen. 3:8–13). They hid from God (v. 8). God called out to Adam and asked if he had eaten from the tree God commanded him not to eat from (vv. 9–11). Adam responded by blaming Eve for his actions and even pointed out that God had given her to be with him (v. 12). By doing this, he partially blamed God too. God asked Eve what it was that she had done, and she blamed the serpent for deceiving her (v. 13). Adam and Eve failed to take full responsibility for their wrongdoing. It was easier to blame someone else for their sinful choices. We do this too, don't we?

Judges 2 lays out the pattern of sin and judgment the Israelites experienced due to their rebellion against God and His clear instructions. In today's reading, God takes responsibility for His people and holds them accountable for their actions. Out of His deep concern and relentless love for them, He testifies against them to expose their disobedience and rebellion.

Imagine a young person you care about is squandering their money and racking up debt on entertainment and extras instead of saving for upcoming expenses. It would be unloving to turn a blind eye to this destructive behavior. It would be loving to address the problem respectfully and help them see the pending consequences for their actions. Keep this example in mind as you interact with today's passage.

## Engage

1. In Judges 2:1, the angel of the Lord reminded the Israelites of these things (fill in the blanks below):

   I brought you out of _____.

   I led you into the _____ I promised to your ancestors.

   I will never break my _____ with you.

2. In Judges 2:2, our focus verse, the people are reminded of these commands they'd been given by God (fill in the blanks below):

   You are not to make a _____ with the

   inhabitants of the land.

   You are to tear down their _____.

   But you have not _____ me.

3. Underline what you learn about Jesus being our Ultimate Deliverer in the following passages.

   **Romans 11:26–27.** "And in this way all Israel will be saved, as it is written, The Deliverer will come from Zion; he will turn god-lessness away from Jacob. And this will be my covenant with them when I take away their sins."

   **Galatians 1:3–4.** "Grace to you and peace from God the Father and our Lord Jesus Christ, who gave himself for our sins to rescue us from this present evil age, according to the will of our God and Father."

### What Have You Done?

In Judges 2:2, God asks His people, "What have you done?"

This is similar to God's question to Adam, "Where are you?" after he and Eve chose to disobey God's clear instructions. God did not ask these things because He was unaware of what happened. He is all-knowing (omniscient). God asked, "Where are you?" and "What have you done?" to show His people that He knew what they had done, and they would have to give an account for it. Why? Because when we fess up, when we admit our wrong, when we acknowledge the gravity of what we have done, we can be changed.

God can forgive, redeem, and restore a repentant sinner. But if we deny, deflect, justify, or blame when confronted with our sin, we are ensnared further and the consequences may need to be more severe to get our attention. Taking responsibility for our actions is a sign of humility and maturity.

In Judges 2:2–3, God's people are being held accountable for their disobedience. God says He will not drive out the Canaanites before them but rather the Canaanites will be thorns, or traps, to them. This sounds harsh, doesn't it? Yet this is a just and loving decision from a holy God. It would be unloving not to hold the Israelites responsible for their actions. It would be unloving not to help them remember the importance of obeying Him. When we experience unpleasant consequences for sin, it helps us to turn from that behavior and choose a better way the next time.

> Taking responsibility for our actions is a sign of humility and maturity.

In the garden of Eden, after Adam and Eve disobeyed God (Gen. 3:14–22), God banished them from the garden. Consider what verse 24 tells us: "He drove the man out and stationed the cherubim and the flaming, whirling sword east of the garden of Eden to guard the way to the tree of life."

God drove Adam and Eve out of the garden not only as a consequence but also as a protection. Since they'd sinned by disobeying His instructions and eating from the tree of the knowledge of good and evil, He did not want them to then eat from the tree of life—and live forever in an eternal state of sin. God was protecting them from permanent separation from Him. God was going to send Jesus to pay the penalty for their sins and our sins so that a new way could be made for us to live forever with Him, not in a sinful state but in a forgiven and redeemed state, unified with Him eternally. Nothing between us.

When God cursed the serpent, He gave a prophetic promise that the woman's child will crush the serpent's head (vv. 14–15). The woman referred to here is Mary, and the child is Jesus.

Adam and Eve made a devastating choice, yet God promised deliverance. Not only did He promise a future deliverance, through Jesus, but God made clothing from skins for Adam and Eve. When they were exposed in their sin and shame, God mercifully clothed them through the sacrifice of an animal. When we are exposed in our sin and shame, God mercifully clothes us through the sacrifice of Jesus's shed blood and His righteousness. He is uncompromising in truth, unrestrained in love.

So, when you read today's passage in Judges, I implore you to read it through the lens of God's fierce care for His people. He did not delight in their suffering but gave them consequences for their actions in order to display His holiness and teach them that obeying Him was best. The judgment they were given exposed their limitations so they would know their desperate need for the Deliverer who could do what they had failed to do: drive out the enemy completely. They needed to be rescued from the snares of sin, to be cleansed so they could be set apart and enjoy their inheritance without evil influence or hindrance.

### God, Have Mercy!

In Judges 2:4, we observe the response of God's people after the angel of the Lord reminded them of His faithfulness and their faithlessness. They wept loudly. They were broken over their sin against a holy God. They had fallen short. They had failed to fully obey. God had kept His end of the covenant; they had broken theirs. The people named this place Bochim, which means "weepers." Through tears, they acknowledged their wrongdoing and took responsibility for their rebellion, offering sacrifices to the Lord for their sin.

In Genesis, God used the skin of dead animals to temporarily cover the sin of Adam and Eve. Based on God's instructions to His people through Moses, the Israelites sacrificed animals on altars repeatedly to atone for their sin. But when Jesus came, He sacrificed Himself on the cross, a pure and spotless lamb, and no more sacrifices were needed for salvation after that. As we continue to follow Jesus, we are called to be a living sacrifice (Rom. 12:1). This is because of His mercy and is meant to set us apart for His purposes. It's not about earning salvation—Jesus already accomplished that. Instead, it's part of our spiritual growth and maturity as we take responsibility for our actions and follow God's guidance.

## Reflect

1. In Judges 2:1, God reminded the people of His faithfulness to them in the past. Jot down the three things God reminded them of, according to this verse.

2. Think about a specific way God has been faithful to you in the past, and write it below.

3. In Judges 2:2–3, God instructed His people to obey Him by staying away from sinful, destructive influences. He compared these influences to a thorn in their sides and a trap. Ask God to show you if there is a sinful, destructive influence in your life. What does He want you to do about this?

4. In Judges 2:4, the people wept loudly because they were convicted about their sin. Ask God to help you grieve over your sin and turn

to His faithful love and lavish mercy as you repent and run into His welcoming arms.

## Bonus

Read Psalm 25 out loud as a prayer to God as you return to the One who loves you best.

---

### DECIDE

When you're trapped by sin, decide to
be responsible for your actions.

## LESSON 2

# "God, What Do I Do with My Influence?"

That whole generation was also gathered to their ancestors.
After them another generation rose up who did not know the
LORD or the works he had done for Israel.

JUDGES 2:10

### Read

JUDGES 2:6–13

Do you want to leave a strong spiritual legacy for your loved ones? One in
which you finish your race well and pass on the baton of faith to the next
generation?

Finishing well doesn't mean running a perfect race. Sometimes we learn
the most from the trip-ups along the way and Father God's forgiveness
welcoming us home. May we grow from our failures and become wiser in
the process.

We have a responsibility to influence others in a way that honors God
and His Word. What we say and do matters. It impacts those we interact
with, whether in person or online. The same is true for what we don't say

or do. What we withhold can also impact those around us. The weight of leaving a godly legacy and influencing others in the ways of God comes into play in Judges 2.

## Focus

God instructed Moses to pass the baton of leadership to Joshua. According to God's directives, Joshua instructed the people to take possession of their allotted territory, their inheritance. The people worshiped the Lord throughout Joshua's lifetime and during the lifetimes of the elders who outlived him. They had a firsthand account of the great works God had done for Israel.

### Dropping the Baton

The focus verse for this lesson grieves me. A whole generation rose up who did not know the Lord or what He had done for their ancestors. In this verse, the word translated "know," *yāḏa'*, refers to being acquainted with God, "involving intelligent worship, obedience."[1] They did not *yāḏa'* God by experience; they did not worship or obey Him.

The two emphasized words in the verses below refer to the same word, *yāḏa'*, in Judges 2:10. The first refers to Pharaoh, in the time of Moses, when God's people were enslaved in Egypt. The second references the rebellious sons of Eli the priest, who judged Israel over two hundred years after the time of Joshua.[2]

> **Exodus 5:2.** "But Pharaoh responded, 'Who is the Lord that I should obey him by letting Israel go? I don't <u>know</u> the Lord, and besides, I will not let Israel go.'"
> **1 Samuel 2:12.** "Eli's sons were wicked men; they did not <u>respect</u> the Lord."

If you read the context of these verses, you discover that Pharaoh and Eli's sons did not know the Lord personally. Their outward behavior demonstrated that their hearts were hardened toward God. Pharaoh lived in a culture and time where the worship of many gods was commonplace. And Eli's sons acted wickedly even though their father served the One True

God. Eli neglected his responsibility to set boundaries for his sons when they disregarded God's commands, and there were grave consequences that resulted in their lives being cut short (1 Sam. 2:27–29, 34).

### Influencing a Generation

What about when the outward behavior looks good, but the heart is still far from the Lord? In Matthew 15:8–9, Jesus says, "These people honor me with their lips, but their hearts are far from me. They worship me in vain; their teachings are merely human rules" (NIV). Jesus is referring to the Pharisees here, calling them out for the discrepancy between what they professed and how they lived.

Some of the most sobering verses in the Bible are found in Matthew 7, when Jesus speaks of those who do things in His name but will not enter the kingdom of heaven because they never knew Him.

> Not everyone who says to me, "Lord, Lord," will enter the kingdom of heaven, but only the one who does the will of my Father in heaven. On that day many will say to me, "Lord, Lord, didn't we prophesy in your name, drive out demons in your name, and do many miracles in your name?" Then I will announce to them, "I never knew you. Depart from me, you lawbreakers!" (vv. 21–23)

The word translated "knew" here is *ginōskō*. The definition is "to 'know' (absolutely). It is 'knowledge grounded on personal experience.'"[3] It seems this is an intimate knowing, indicating a reciprocal relationship. So, when Jesus says, "I never knew you," it reveals we can do things for Jesus but still not really know Him. In other words, we can know about Him, show up in church, donate to the poor, yet not really know Him personally as our Lord. These are hard truths to swallow, but I would rather choke them down than discard them because the ramifications impact us and others, both now and for eternity.

If our actions are disobedient to God's commands, those around us will find reasons to justify their sin or discount their need to follow biblical Jesus in daily life. Or, if our actions are admirable yet our hearts are far from God, the next generation will see right through that. They can sniff out hypocrisy and duplicity from a mile away. If we want to influence a generation effectively for God's kingdom, we need to know Jesus intimately ourselves. We can't pass on what we haven't first received and put into practice.

God clearly instructed His people not to keep silent but to tell the next generation of His praise-worthy deeds, His power, and the wonders He had done. "They were to rise and tell their children" (Ps. 78:6) so they might know Him and not be stubborn or rebellious but put their confidence in God, not forgetting His works or failing to keep His commands (vv. 4–8).

> If we want to influence a generation effectively for God's kingdom, we need to know Jesus intimately ourselves. We can't pass on what we haven't first received and put into practice.

God instructed His people to teach their children about Him as they went about their day—when they sat, when they rose, when they walked, when they slept (Deut. 11:19). My friend Charity does this with her six children; they walk their neighborhood daily and talk about the things of God. As they move their feet, they process questions and hurts and celebrate successes through the lens of God's Word. Passing on your faith doesn't have to be complicated, but it requires intention—day by day, step by step, conversation after conversation.

The Israelites neglected this important task of passing on faith to their children, and the results were catastrophic. *The Moody Bible Commentary* expounds,

> This unfortunate failure of the people over time to educate their own children contributed to many of the moral and spiritual breakdowns of Israel during this era. The contrast between those who served the Lord ([Judg.] 2:7) and those who served the Baals (2:11) is striking. The essence of godliness is a willingness to submit to *the* King, that is, the Lord of Israel, but the essence of sinfulness is a growing willingness to submit to the gods of the nations.[4]

We see this happening in our lifetime too, don't we? Maybe even in our own homes? Let's pause and pray together.

*Dear God, forgive us for not taking our responsibility as seriously as we should in telling the next generation about who You are, who they are in*

*You, and the miraculous things You have done for us. Show us how to be faithful in this area. Teach us how to teach them Your ways and Your truth. We want the next generation to encounter You for themselves. May they be faithful to tell their friends, their children, and their grand-children about You also. May no generation neglect their responsibility to share the Good News of the gospel and the specific ways You have de-livered them. There is much at stake. Thank You for providing the help we need to carry out Your clear instructions. In Jesus's name, Amen.*

No matter your status, you have influence over someone. Your words, actions, social media posts and shares, alliances, and stances all impact others.

## Engage

1. Read the following verses and record what you learn about being influenced and influencing others.

Deuteronomy 32:45–47

Proverbs 13:20

Proverbs 14:26–27

Psalm 145:4–7, 11–13

2. Judges 2:11–13 describes how the generation that did not know the Lord behaved. Underline the verbs (action words) in the passage to see what God's people did.

- The Israelites did what was evil in the Lᴏʀᴅ's sight.
- They worshiped the Baals.
- They abandoned the Lᴏʀᴅ, the God of their ancestors, who had brought them out of Egypt.
- They followed other gods from the surrounding peoples and bowed down to them.
- They angered the Lᴏʀᴅ.
- They abandoned him and worshiped Baal and the Ashtoreths.

Baal was the main god of the Canaanite nations. He was tied to sun and storms. Ashtoreth was the main goddess of the Canaanite nations. She was tied to sex and fertility. The worship of Baal and Ashtoreth was "grossly licentious and cruel and included animal sacrifices, male and female prostitution, and sometimes human sacrifices, things that should never have been referred to as worship!"[5] Worshiping false gods brings death to your soul as you toil to fill a bottomless pit and appease a moving target. Christ offers life; pagan worship brings death.

3. The last chapter of Joshua, which is right before the book of Judges, warns God's people what would happen if they abandoned God. Take some time to read Joshua 24:14–28. Jot down a verse or two that stands out to you from this passage:

In Judges 2:12 and 2:13 we see the word *abandoned*. Basically, they left behind, deserted, or cast off the Lord and followed other gods. Why? Was God lacking? Had He not proven His power to them time and time again? Did they not like His commands? Did they not believe God?

Joshua clearly instructed the people about what would happen if they abandoned the Lord. So why did they not warn the next generation about what would transpire if they forsook the Lord and His way?

As we see in Judges 2:11–13, things did not go well for those who did not know God or His mighty works. They were influenced by the culture around them instead of carrying out the commands of God. Remember, His commands were for their good as well as for their protection. They were not arbitrary restrictions but divine wisdom.

## Reflect

1. Do you view God's commands as suggestions or as statutes? Why do you think that is?

2. Do you view God's commands as restrictive or life-giving? Why do you think that is?

3. Who are some of the people who have influenced you the most along your faith journey?

4. How has their example specifically helped shape you?

## Bonus

Read 2 Peter 3:17 as a blessing and exhortation as you decide to take responsibility for the way you are being influenced and how you are influencing others.

**DECIDE**

When you aren't sure what to do with your influence, decide to be responsible with your impact on others.

# "God, What Do I Do When I Suffer?"

Whenever the Israelites went out, the LORD was against them and brought disaster on them, just as he had promised and sworn to them. So they suffered greatly.

JUDGES 2:15

## Read

JUDGES 2:14–15

Suffering is a part of life, a reality of living in these present times. Some of us might want to pretend suffering is not a part of the Christian life, and others may be so familiar with it that they can't remember what it is like to live without it. In some form or fashion, we have all experienced suffering or will experience it. As we read in Judges 2, God's people suffered greatly.

## Focus

The Lord's anger burned against Israel because they ignored all His instructions. They were wise in their own eyes and did not fear Him as they should. As a result, He handed them over to raiders. He sold them to their enemies, and they could no longer resist them. Whenever the Israelites went forth, the Lord was against them and brought disaster upon them, as He promised and swore that He would.

If we choose not to take responsibility for our actions or our influence, God may use difficult circumstances and other people to hold us responsible and grow us in humility. Again, this is not out of malicious intent but out of deep concern and steadfast love. Don't hear me as saying that any and all suffering we experience is a consequence for sinful behavior. It is not. We live in a fallen world, and sometimes bad things happen because of it. Sometimes the suffering we experience is a direct result of doing something *right*. For example, we read in the New Testament about how Jesus's disciples were met with persecution and torturous deaths. In the Old Testament we read how Job faithfully followed God, but God sovereignly allowed him to be severely tested.

In summary, when we experience suffering, it could be:

* A consequence for sin (Rom. 5:12–21).
* The result of living in a fallen world (John 9:1–7).
* An indication we are obeying the Lord (John 15:18–25).

For example, if we steal something, a consequence might be prosecution for shoplifting. If we break an ankle falling down the stairs, it could simply be a result of living in a fallen world (pun intended). Or if we endure a long season of waiting, it might be God's way of refining us so we don't become prideful when He entrusts us with more.

> Regardless of the reason for our suffering, Christ can be glorified in it and change us through it.

We may not know the specific reasons for our suffering, but we can rest assured that our suffering does not go unnoticed by God. He is well aware of everything that concerns us and promises to be with us in it. We don't have to wait until we are at the end of our suffering to draw near to God. He is in the midst of it, with us. Often, He is working a greater purpose, beyond what we can even imagine, in our struggles. Regardless of the reason for our suffering, Christ can be glorified and change us through it.

## Engage

1. By way of review, circle the letter that gives the reason for the Israelites' suffering in Judges 2 (hint: vv. 11–12).

   A. A consequence for their sin.
   B. The result of living in a fallen world.
   C. An indication they were obeying the Lord.

   In today's passage, it is clear that the Israelites were suffering because of their sin against holy God. Judges 2:14–15 outlines the specific consequences God gave the Israelites for their disobedience. Keep in mind, they had been warned these things would happen if they did not follow His commands. They chose not to obey God, and so He delivered these consequences to them.

2. Read Judges 2:14 and fill in the details:

   The Lord's anger _____ against

   _____ .

   He _____ them over to marauders who raided them.

   He _____ them to the enemies around them.

   The result? They could no longer _____ their enemies.

   It can be easy to focus on the result of the Lord's anger, but why was He angry? What drove His anger? What Scripture supports your answer?

### Stand Strong

God uses our suffering to grow us and transform us. Often the struggles we face are fertile ground to grow our faith muscles so we can stand strong in the coming days.

> Often the struggles we face are fertile ground to grow our faith muscles so we can stand strong in the coming days.

As hard as the suffering may be, our Savior can empathize with us and has suffered far beyond what we can fathom. Jesus took the weight of the sin of the whole world—past, present, and future—upon Himself. He bore our punishment. And He had done nothing wrong. Jesus suffered more than anyone ever has, is, or will. His endurance and His character were tested to the outer limits so that we might have eternal hope through Him.

It is tempting when we are suffering to despair, to question, to shake our fists, yet suffering can bring great gain—if we let it. Trying times are not fun, but they forge things into our character that cannot easily be snatched away. As we come forth as gold through the refining process, we are positioned to offer a balm of comfort to those who are hurting around us. Nothing is wasted.

### By the Spirit

Romans 8:12–14 reminds us of how God's children are to behave. Whether we are in a time of plenty or need, a time of clarity or indecision, or a time of success or failure, we are to walk by the Spirit, not the flesh. Romans 8:15 reminds those who are His not to give way to fear but to "cry out 'Abba, Father!'" to the God who has adopted us into His family. We can be secure in our sense of belonging and our inheritance, and have comfort in following a Savior who suffered and who can be glorified when we suffer *with* Him. Never alone. "The Spirit himself testifies together with our spirit that we are God's children, and if children, also heirs—heirs of God and coheirs with Christ—if indeed we suffer with him so that we may also be glorified with him" (vv. 16–17).

God's people experienced consequences for their disobedience in Judges 2:14–15. They were given a gracious opportunity to repent, grow in humility, and experience godly transformation. Trials are opportunities to draw closer to the tender care, incomparable comfort, and unchanging holiness of Jesus. Whether the difficulty you face is a result of sin, the reality of living in a falling world, or a result of faithfully following Christ, it can fortify your faith so that even when the earth gives way, you are found standing on the Rock, through His strength and for His glory.

## Reflect

1. What is a current struggle you have?

2. In what ways is this suffering producing endurance and character in your life? If you aren't sure, talk to God about this and listen for His insight.

## Bonus

As you finish today's lesson, read Psalm 46. Write down a verse or two to cling to in uncertain times.

**DECIDE**

When you suffer, decide to be a responsible follower of Christ who views suffering as an opportunity to grow in humility and experience godly transformation.

# "God, What Do I Do When I'm Tempted to Judge?"

Whenever the LORD raised up a judge for the Israelites, the LORD was with him and saved the people from the power of their enemies while the judge was still alive. The LORD was moved to pity whenever they groaned because of those who were oppressing and afflicting them.

JUDGES 2:18

## Read

JUDGES 2:16–19

It's no fun to be judged, especially unfairly. Yet we can be quick to judge others.

When my family lived in a hotel for 102 days, after a partial house flood, my kids enjoyed watching *Judge Judy*. Don't judge; we were trying to survive a strange time in our family history. The kids enjoyed Judy's straightforward approach and how she put people in their place. The biblical judges we are studying had a similar direct approach, but their role was quite different.

## Focus

The Israelites' judges were not like those in a courtroom but rather were regional rulers, a type of military leader or deliverer who addressed the threat of the surrounding nations. These judges were raised up by God to carry out His purposes and govern the people in that particular region. It is likely that some of these judges were alive at the same time, overseeing various portions of the Promised Land.

In Judges 2:19, we read, "Whenever the judge died, the Israelites would act even more corruptly than their ancestors, following other gods to serve them and bow in worship to them. They did not turn from their evil practices or their obstinate ways." In verse 18 we see a key repeated phrase that we first saw in Judges 1: "the LORD was *with* him" (emphasis added). Even as the Israelites faced difficulties brought on by their own disobedience, the Lord was present by being *with* the judge who presided over them. God raised up judges to save the Israelites from the power of their enemies.

> Don't discount the power of God's presence or underestimate His sovereign plan—even when you don't like the plan.

The Israelites' struggle against their enemies was allowed by God for His greater purposes. The struggle didn't mean they weren't loved or had been abandoned. God mercifully provided judges for His people as a form of relief for them in the midst of their self-induced predicament. Don't discount the power of God's presence or underestimate His sovereign plan—even when you don't like the plan.

Even though the Lord raised up judges to save the Israelites from the power of the raiders, they acted corruptly.

## Engage

Use the word bank to fill in the answers below, based on Judges 2:17:

gods   listen   obedience   ancestors (use 2×)

1. They did not _____ to their judges.

2. They prostituted themselves with other _____, bowing

   down to them.

3. They quickly turned from the way of their _____,

   who had walked in _____ to the Lord's

   commands.

4. They did not do as their _____ did.

### When No One Is Watching

The end of Judges 2:18 says, "The Lord was moved to pity whenever they groaned because of those who were oppressing and afflicting them." Even though the Israelites blatantly rebelled against God, He was compassionate toward them. He saw them. He provided a way to ease their burden—that had been brought on by their sin—by raising up judges to govern over them. The people disregarded the wisdom of the most responsible and accurate Judge. They proved they could not govern themselves without an overseer, yet He graciously offered them oversight in the form of these judges.

The other day I had a conversation with one of my older children in which I said something like this: "Whether I am at home or in town, it is expected that you obey my instructions. The rules still apply even if I am not here." It is part of my responsibility as a parent to do what I can to forge my children's character so they are positioned for success instead of destruction, according to God's truth. I cannot choose for them, but I can clearly point them to Him with my words and actions.

A sign hangs in our home based on a famous quote by former UCLA basketball coach John Wooden: "The true test of a man's character is what he does when no one is watching." We see this concept played out with the Israelites. God raised up judges to help spare them from both moral and military destruction. But whenever the judge died, the Israelites went right back to their sinful practices. They acted like their ancestors, following other gods, serving them, and bowing down in worship to them. They did not repent of their wicked, stubborn ways. They continued in their rebellion instead of guarding the liberty they had been given through the judge (v. 19). In other words, when the judge was not there as a tangible reminder to do things God's way, they stopped doing the right thing. Out of sight, out of mind.

### Judgy-Wudgy

It is tempting to take on the role of judge. Out of genuine concern or out of pride, we may be tempted to try to micromanage the decisions of those around us. It can be maddening when our well-intended advice is disregarded or mocked. If only so and so would listen to us and all our wisdom, they would be spared from heartache.

As I run for school board, I find myself being judged unfairly and judging unfairly. Sometimes we don't have all the facts, and sometimes we make snap judgments based on a partial view of something we don't fully understand. What is the remedy for this? When we are tempted to puff ourselves up, thinking we know best, it is crucial to revere God and His role as the only perfect Judge. He knows everything; nothing is hidden from Him to whom we must give an account (Heb. 4:13). May we live in the Spirit according to God's standards, with the power and wisdom He supplies (1 Pet. 4:6).

## Reflect

1. Look up the following verses and record what they say about God being our Judge. Don't skip over these passages; they are life-giving water to grow your understanding about this important attribute of God. This is definitely not an exhaustive list. If you have time, look up more verses about God as Judge to obtain a more robust understanding of this aspect of His character.

   Isaiah 33:22

Psalm 9:7–10

James 4:11–12

2 Timothy 4:1–8

Revelation 20:11–15

2. After reading the verses above, what is a correction you might need
   to make in your thinking about God as Judge?

There are times when a correct judgment changes us and when it spares
us from continued heartache.

## Bonus

Take some time to confess the times you have been quick to judge instead
of trusting God to judge. Be specific and receive God's forgiveness. Pray
for those who do not yet know Jesus as their Savior and that God would
help you love them like He does.

## DECIDE

When you're tempted to judge, decide to revere
God as a responsible and accurate Judge.

# "God, What Do I Do When Life Feels Heavy?"

I did this to test Israel and to see whether or not they would keep the LORD's way by walking in it, as their ancestors had.

JUDGES 2:22

## Read

JUDGES 2:20–23

Things can go from bad to worse in an instant. How do we hold hope when life feels so heavy that we fear we will be crushed under the weight of it? How do we manage the demands of life without compromise? We need God's help to stay faithful when we are suffering. We are desperate for His intervention. We require His help to uphold a covenant relationship when our hearts are enticed by the lure of the sinful world and its false promises of fulfillment. When we can't see the way forward, we cry out to the Holy One for hope.

## Focus

In the first part of Judges 2:20, we read about the Lord's anger burning against Israel. Because He is holy and just, He judges His people with equity (Ps. 98:9). Let's not miss what it says next: "this nation has violated my covenant that I made with their ancestors and disobeyed me" (Judg. 2:20). The word *covenant* here is crucial.

Covenant is not something to be entered into lightly. In Scripture, sometimes *covenant* is defined as "an agreement, a mutual undertaking, between God and Israel" like a commandment, and sometimes it refers to "a promise or undertaking on the part of God."[1] Covenant means there is nothing that will separate us, not even death. Sounds like marriage vows, doesn't it? Time and time again, the Israelites were unfaithful to the covenant that God made with their ancestors through their disobedience to His commands and their deplorable acts of pagan worship.

## Engage

1. Keep these different definitions of *covenant* in mind as you read, study, and record what you learn about the word in these verses.

   Deuteronomy 7:7–16

   Psalm 103:13–18

Hebrews 8:6–13

### Training for Your Reigning

Queen Elizabeth II passed away in 2022 at the age of ninety-six. She reigned as queen of the United Kingdom for seven decades and appointed fifteen prime ministers. What a legacy of commitment and endurance. Elizabeth was crowned queen at the age of twenty-seven. She accepted her new position not only by receiving the title but by assuming the responsibilities that came with it. She took her duty seriously and did not waver.

More impressive than Queen Elizabeth's devotion to her role as sovereign is Jesus's devotion to His covenant with His people as King of kings. He did not fail them. He kept up His end of the covenant. Jesus invites you into a covenant relationship too, one in which He upholds His promise to save you from sin's destruction (Ps. 103:1–5), set you apart to become more like Him (1 John 2:3–6), and keep you until He returns and you reign eternally with Him (2 Tim. 2:8–13).

I have no idea of the incredible weight Elizabeth must have felt as she carried out her lofty assignment, but I have a minuscule idea about what it feels like to be asked to rise to a task that feels beyond your strength and threatens to crush you with the weight of its honorable duty. For me, it has been running for school board. The other day I was tested in my resolve as someone on social media assumed negative things about my character because I did not respond in the way they thought I should. I'm pretty sure the Queen had entire countries upset with her at one time or another.

As my heart pounded and my mind swirled from this person's comments, God reminded me of a phrase my friend Dawn often says: "This is training for your reigning." It brought comfort to know that this circumstance, which God allowed, was a strengthening exercise. He knows what will be required of each of us in our present and future roles, and He does not want us to be unprepared. God provides training and strengthening so we are better equipped for what is coming.

We see God do the same in Judges 2:20–23. He knows that suffering can increase our faith more than seasons of ease can. He allows circumstances to test and refine us. He knows exactly what kinds of stamina and wisdom will be required for our future assignments. The Lord loves us too much to leave us untrained. In our focus verse for today, Judges 2:22, it says, "I did this to test Israel and to see whether or not they would keep the LORD's way by walking in it, as their ancestors had." God knew His people would not pass the test. The Lord left the nations that His people had not driven out immediately to see if they would keep His way or not, as their ancestors had. It is interesting to note that Scripture says He did this to see if they would keep His way by *walking* in it. Keeping the Lord's way is not a passive activity but an active one. It requires applying what has been learned, not simply knowing about it but moving in the direction God lays out like a map, through His instructions in the Bible and the leading of the Holy Spirit.

> Each task, each trial, each decision faced is training for your future reigning with Christ, the King of kings.

Whatever weighty call you are answering, whether it is caring for a sick loved one, enduring a demanding work situation, parenting small children, fighting for justice, or leading a company, it helps to remember that each task, each trial, each decision faced is training for your future reigning with Christ, the King of kings (Dan. 7:18, 27).

### Consider It All Joy

All Scripture is God-breathed (2 Tim. 3:16–17), yet some verses are harder to rally behind than others (even though they are true). Take James 1:2–4, for example: "Consider it a great joy, my brothers and sisters, whenever you experience various trials, because you know that the testing of your faith produces endurance. And let endurance have its full effect, so that you may be mature and complete, lacking nothing."

Consider it a great joy when we experience trials? Joy is not often our go-to in difficult times, is it? But it is true: the testing of our faith is a gift. No one wants to face battles with atrophied faith. In other words, we don't want to lose our faith's "effectiveness or vigor due to underuse or neglect."[2] The testing might not feel good, but it can be used *for* good.

Throughout Scripture, we read examples of people being tested, not because God is cruel but because He is holy and loving. He allows circumstances in our lives that point us to our need for constant dependence on Him. As we lean into Him, we discover that He will uphold and sustain us and we develop a strong faith, which is a priceless, essential gift.

## Reflect

1. Reread James 1:2–4 and use the word bank below to fill in the blanks to help you remember that testing in your life can bring about good.

> mature   endurance (use 2×)   nothing   complete

The testing of your faith produces _____.

And let _____ have its

full effect, so that you may be _____ and

_____, lacking _____.

2. Who is someone from history who inspires you regarding the way they endured in difficulties?

3. What is one action you can take to demonstrate endurance today?

## Bonus

Read Psalm 98, then write out your own prayer of thanks for who God is and what He does. Ask Him to help you accept and apply what you learn in this passage.

---

**DECIDE**

When life feels heavy, decide to be
a responsible Christ-follower who reads, accepts,
and applies what they learn from God's Word.

---

*Dear Jesus,*

*Thank You for taking responsibility for us when we rebelled against God. You did nothing wrong. Thank You for carrying the heaviest load—our sin to the cross—dying a criminal's death so that we could be saved. You made a way so we can walk in Your light and not be crushed under the weight of the world. We are changed because You have risen again in power and make us new through the forgiveness of our sins. We want to be trustworthy with the redeemed life You have given us. We want to influence others toward You, not repel them, but we need Your help to do so. Thank You for interceding for us. Suffering is a part of this fallen world, but You are right here with us, forging our character and sharpening our faith as we walk through difficulties. You can redeem anything and anyone, including us.*

*Thank You for modeling what it means to love others and care for them right where they are. Multiply our capacity to love. May we apply what we learn in the Bible and not only know it but live it. May we be faithful followers of You, dependable and responsible to seek You, follow You, and care for those around us with the strength You provide. Thank You for taking such good care of us. Amen.*

# WEEK 2 WRAP-UP

*This week, I decide to be responsible
with my thoughts, actions, and influence.*

Answer the following questions to help summarize what you learned during this week of study. If possible, use biblical references to back up your responses.

1. What is your main responsibility as a follower of Christ?

2. In this season of your life, what is one of your main responsibilities?

3. How does the Bible define *responsibility*, based on the Scriptures you read this week?

4. In what ways does God take care of you?

5. Based on what you discovered in Lessons 1–5, how can the decision to be responsible help you make wise decisions in uncertain times?

# THE DECISION TO ENDURE

## JUDGES 3

Now that we understand what it means to be a responsible Christ-follower and how irresponsible choices can trap us, holding us back from peaceful, abundant living, it's time to dig into Judges 3. This week of study will focus on the accounts of some of the judges God installed to govern Israel and how their perseverance ushered in breakthrough. You will discover that the decision to endure is crucial as you fulfill your unique purpose at this time in history and choose to keep following God's lead each day.

**KEY VERSE: JAMES 1:4**

And let endurance have its full effect, so that you may be mature and complete, lacking nothing.

# "God, What Do I Do When I'm Tested?"

This was to teach the future generations of the Israelites how to fight in battle, especially those who had not fought before.

JUDGES 3:2

## Read

JUDGES 3:1–6

Like squawking seagulls begging for breadcrumbs, small children incessantly ask *why*. And sometimes we do the same: "*Why* have You allowed this, God?" "*Why* won't You come through in that way I want You to, God?" "*Why* do I have to face this, God?" Judges 3:1 reiterates that the Lord left the nations to test Israel and then, in verse 2, He tells us why. This testing was to teach the future generations of the Israelites how to fight in battle, especially those who had not fought before.

Again, we see God's kindness to prepare them, and us, for difficulties ahead. God tested His people to prepare and train those who did not have much experience in battle. They needed to know how to stand upon the firm foundation of God's instructions in the face of resistance—how to fight, how to be proactive, and how to endure under pressure. If we want to endure when tested, we need to be trained to use these spiritual weapons.

## Focus

Endurance is not quickly developed. It takes consistency over time. It takes staying. It requires leaning into God's comfort and carrying out His commands in the presence of difficulties, waiting longer than you want to, and taking the necessary steps to build and fortify what will be required for the coming days. It takes foresight and bold belief.

> Endurance is not quickly developed. It takes consistency over time. It takes staying.

Western culture often idolizes comfort, ease, and security. But when faced with opposition, injustice, and trials, how should we respond? How do we contend for the faith in adversity? It is tempting to listen to the doubters, and to the accuser, when life feels unpredictable and unstable. Like the Israelites needed to be equipped and prepare for battle, we need to be outfitted with supernatural weapons to temper our fleshly reactions and extinguish the fiery darts of the enemy.

Ephesians 6:10–20 outlines the armor of God that believers have been supplied for battle and for everyday life:

**Helmet of salvation.** Putting on the helmet is fully receiving your salvation, through acceptance of Jesus's work on the cross. It's having the mind of Christ, taking your thoughts captive in obedience to God's Word.

**Breastplate of righteousness.** Receiving His righteousness, made possible through Jesus's forgiveness, you are dependent on His sacrificial love and guard your new identity as God's son or daughter, and He continues to mature you.

**Shield of faith.** You take up this protection welded by belief, trust, and confidence in Jesus, His power, and His promises. This weapon deflects what is thrown at you as you move forward with assurance that God has no equal.

**Belt of truth.** Knowing the Word, you wrap it securely around you to uphold you and shore up your convictions.

**Sword of the Spirit.** You actively and accurately apply the Word of God to situations you encounter.

**Sandals of peace.** You have a readiness to take the gospel of peace, which offers reconciliation to God through Christ, to those around you. The kind of peace mentioned here is "the tranquil state of a soul assured of its salvation through Christ, and so fearing nothing from God and content with its earthly lot, of whatsoever sort that is."[1]

## Engage

1. Read Ephesians 6:10–20 and answer the following questions:

(Verse 10) Where does your strength come from?

(Verse 11) What are you to put on, and why are you to put it on?

(Verse 12) What is your struggle not against, and what is your struggle against?

(Verse 13) You are to put on the full armor of God, so that you can

_____ in the evil day and take your _____ .

(Verses 14–17) The six pieces of armor are mentioned in these
verses. Which one of them do you want to learn more about,
and why?

(Verse 18) What instructions are given about prayer?

(Verses 19–20) What does Paul ask for prayer about?

2. In what ways can we put on the full armor of God? In other words, what does it look like in our daily life to put on the belt of truth, breastplate of righteousness, sandals of peace, shield of faith, helmet of salvation, and sword of the Spirit?

3. These pieces of armor are impenetrable aspects of Jesus. He is our salvation, our righteousness, the truth that girds us, the gospel of peace, our shield of faith, and the Word of God. These pieces of armor are not things we obtain apart from Jesus; they are gifted to us by Him. It would be foolish to ignore or fail to utilize what has been given to us for protection as we battle this present darkness. How might this change your approach to putting on the armor? Read Romans 13:11–14 and record your conclusion below. What are you to put on?

### *Weapons of Warfare*

Paul writes in 2 Corinthians 10:3–5,

For although we live in the flesh, we do not wage war according to the flesh, since the weapons of our warfare are not of the flesh, but are powerful through God for the demolition of strongholds. We demolish arguments and every proud thing that is raised up against the knowledge of God, and we take every thought captive to obey Christ.

I have heard it explained that the weapons of our warfare are the Word of God, prayer, worship, Jesus's name, fasting, our testimony, and thanksgiving.[2] I want to be fully equipped with the armor of God and these powerful weapons in order to stand strong with the Lord, in His mighty power, and finish this race well.

Look up the following Scriptures (bonus: if you have time, write them down too) and record what you learn in order to solidify why these spiritual practices are powerful weapons to help us stand strong in our faith in Jesus.

1. **God's Word:** Hebrews 4:12

2. **Prayer:** James 5:13–16

3. **Worship:** 2 Chronicles 20:20–22

4. **The name of Jesus:** Acts 4:8–12

5. **Fasting:** Mark 9:25–29

6. **Your testimony:** Revelation 12:9–11

7. **Thanksgiving:** Psalm 50:14–15

### *Stand Firm*

God clearly lays out in His Word that this is how we contend for the faith from generation to generation, until Jesus returns. With the power of the Holy Spirit, God's full armor, and His weapons of warfare, we are equipped to stand firm in trying times. How kind of God to clearly train us how to fight in battle. This armor and these weapons are proven, countercultural methods for engaging in war. They offer us wisdom, authority, and spiritual perspective to face the coming days.

We are given choices every day: we can endure or give up, wake up to what is happening around us or live in denial, and choose wisdom or foolishness. With the strength God supplies, in the spiritual battle that rages here on earth, we can operate in the Spirit—or we can resolve to let our fleshly desires lead, settle for less than God's best, be wise in our own eyes, and disregard the Lord and His commands. Those commands that are for our good and for our flourishing.

In Judges 3:5–6 we read that those God tested, the ones He gave an opportunity to be trained for battle, settled into what was comfortable instead of carrying out what was right by obeying the One True God's commands. Hear what the text says as you think on this: "But they settled among the Canaanites, Hethites, Amorites, Perizzites, Hivites, and Jebusites. The Israelites took their daughters as wives for themselves, gave their own daughters to their sons, and worshiped their gods." Their settling didn't display contentment in God's plan or show them putting down roots based on His lead; rather they rooted themselves in compromise and rebellion and did not resist the lure of the godless cultures around them.

I have to be honest; I'm getting weary of reading about God's people not obeying Him, aren't you? When will they learn and turn from their stubborn ways and admit that He knows best and His commands are for their good? But even as I vent my frustration, I am convicted that I am often like them. Thankfully, we have not been left to fend for ourselves! Jesus, our Great Deliverer, has already come to save us from our failings, and the Holy Spirit abides within us, reminding us of Jesus's words and empowering us to endure.

The entirety of the Bible is given to lovingly instruct us, to help us know the Lord more. So even though I really want to read in Judges that God's people turned from their wickedness and fully embraced God's ways, I know their recorded failings are a warning and a road map, urgently pointing us to our desperate need for Jesus. The Israelites were not left without hope, and neither are we. God has graciously, wisely provided what we need to endure today.

### Reflect

1. Read Romans 10:9–13, which clearly outlines the gospel. Write this passage out below.

In Ephesians 6:20, Paul ends by saying, "Pray that I may declare [the gospel] fearlessly, as I should" (NIV). Based on the passage, answer the following questions.

2. What are some of your fears about sharing the gospel?

3. What is at stake if you choose not to share the gospel with others?

### Bonus

Look over the lists of the armor of God and the spiritual weapons of warfare. Which one of these do you need/want to grow in the most right now? What is one action you can take today to practice using this tool more effectively?

**DECIDE**

When you are tested, decide to endure with the armor of God and His weapons of warfare.

## LESSON 2

# "God, What Do I Do When I'm in a Battle?"

### ▓ Othniel: The First Judge

The Israelites cried out to the LORD. So the LORD raised up Othniel son of Kenaz, Caleb's youngest brother, as a deliverer to save the Israelites.

JUDGES 3:9

**Read**

JUDGES 3:7–11

We don't have to look far to recognize we are in a battle—a battle for truth, a fight for hope, a war against deception. What can we do about it? How do we avoid rebellion in our own hearts as it becomes more difficult to live out our faith in a hostile culture? Let's gain wisdom from the truths packed in Judges 3.

## Focus

Othniel was the first judge whom God raised up for His people, in Judges 3. We will also take a look at two more judges this week, Ehud and Shamgar. The Israelites had the opportunity to be led by God alone: the perfect Judge, King, and Sovereign. Yet they chose to resist His rightful authority and quickly found themselves in trouble.

In Judges 3:7, we read that "The Israelites did what was evil in the LORD's sight; they forgot the LORD their God and worshiped the Baals and the Asherahs." Israel was a chosen people, a nation set apart for God and His purposes. They were in a covenant (a legally binding agreement) with Him, yet they were unfaithful to their faithful God. They did not live for God, nor did they live from the identity God had given them. They began to behave badly, like the nations around them.

Doing whatever you want might sound fun, and even feel fun, yet if your choices are in opposition to God's ways, they lead to enslavement. Disobedience leads to bondage. You may not feel the effects at first, but, in 1 Samuel 15:22–23, God's Word clearly spells out that rebellion against Him is like the sin of witchcraft. This is serious!

The Lord had instructed Saul, through the prophet Samuel, to completely destroy the Amalekites because of how they had opposed the Israelites along the way as they were coming out of Egypt (1 Sam. 15:1–3). Saul did not fully obey the Lord and, when confronted about this by Samuel, responded by deflecting, blaming, and twisting the truth to make himself look better. A similar strategy was used by Adam and Eve in the garden when they sinned against God.

Saul's failure to fully obey God serves as a sober warning about the seriousness of sin.

## Engage

You may be thinking, *How is anyone able to measure up to God's holy standard when it's so easy to fall short?* The most effective way is tucked in the following passage.

1. Read Judges 3:9–11 and fill in the blanks to discover the relief the Israelites were mercifully given, even in the midst of their forgetfulness, falling short, and idol worship.

   (Verse 9) They cried out to _____ .

   (Verse 9) God raised up _____

   son of _____ , who was

   _____ 's youngest brother.

   (Verse 9) Othniel's role was a _____ ,

   to _____ the Israelites.

   (Verse 10) The _____ of the LORD came on

   him and he _____ Israel.

   (Verse 10) Othniel went out to battle, and the

   _____ handed over King Cushan-rishathaim

   of _____ to him, so that Othniel

   _____ him.

   (Verse 11) Then the land had _____

   for _____ years, and Othniel son of

   _____ died.

2. It is interesting to note that Othniel was already mentioned in Judges 1. He is the son of Caleb's youngest brother. Reread Judges 1:12–14 to review and record what you've already learned about Othniel.

3. Look again at Judges 3:10. Who came upon Othniel?

How many of us are trying to work harder and do better, yet we have forgotten or bypassed the true source of power?

In Lesson 4 of Week 2, I mentioned the major life interruption our family of seven experienced as a result of a flood. We were overjoyed to move back into our home after the repairs were finally completed. I assumed we would pick up where we left off and enjoy our restored home in peace. I was wrong. We soon found ourselves in a battle of wills. After a while, my husband and I sensed there was more going on than the stress of our displacement and return. We were in spiritual battle, and supernatural intervention was needed more than lectures. We interceded on behalf of our family, exerting our God-given authority instead of standing back while the accuser tried to divide us. The Holy Spirit broke through hardened ground. Trusted friends joined us in prayer, and the darkness started to roll back.

We continue to agree with God in prayer that He will restore the brokenness completely one day. Our responsibility is to agree with Him and hold the line, deflecting those fiery darts with the shield of faith.

Sometimes we face battles that are beyond our strength, but they are never beyond God's. If the battle ahead threatens to dissipate your resolve, cling to the truth found in Psalm 32:6–7:

> Therefore let everyone who is faithful pray to you immediately.
> When great floodwaters come,
> they will not reach him.
> You are my hiding place;
> you protect me from trouble.
> You surround me with joyful shouts of deliverance.

If we are going to endure and overcome in this life, operating from and through the Holy Spirit is a must. Othniel was able to fulfill his sacred assignment to judge Israel because the Holy Spirit enabled him. Listen to how Matthew Henry addresses this aspect of the text:

> He first judged Israel, reproved them, called them to an account for their sins, and reformed them, and then went out to war. This was the right method. Let sin at home be conquered, that worst of enemies, and then enemies abroad will be more easily dealt with. Thus let Christ be our Judge and Law-giver, and then *he will save us*, and on no others' terms (Isa. 33:22).[1]

Othniel went out to battle, and the Lord gave him success. He was able to overpower King Cushan-rishathaim of Aram because the Holy Spirit directed and empowered him. The result of his obedience and submission to the Spirit was this: the land had peace for forty years (Judg. 3:11).

When we call out for peace in our chaos-ridden circumstances, sometimes the answer is a fight—a fight to contend for the faith.

> Othniel was able to fulfill his sacred assignment to judge Israel because the Holy Spirit enabled him.

## Figure 3.1: Contend for the Faith

**Repent** ⟶ **Return** ⟶ **Realign**
of your sin        to God        your mind
Psalm 51.4        1 Peter 2:25        Romans 12:2

**Repent** of your error (Ps. 51:4).

**Return** to the Overseer of your soul (1 Pet. 2:25).

**Realign** your mind and heart to the ways of God (Rom. 12:2).

*Dear God, I have wandered from Your ways. I desire to walk in a way that honors You. Thank You that You offer Your Holy Spirit to enable me to repent of sin, return to You, and realign with truth. Give me hope in this moment, Father God. Remind me of Your ability in my weakness, Your provision for my lack, Your compassion on my hardest days. I need You, Jesus! Holy Spirit, empower me to walk in Your ways each day—to obey with joy, to endure with courage, to overcome through the victory You have already won. Amen.*

## Reflect

As you finish today's lesson, read through Jude 17–25. Pay special attention to what you learn about the Trinity (the Holy Spirit, Jesus, and God the Father). Record what you discover in Jude below.

*For example: When we pray in the Holy Spirit, we are built up in our faith and don't follow ungodly desires (vv. 18, 20).*

Holy Spirit:

Jesus:

God the Father:

## Bonus

Read 1 Samuel 15 in its entirety to better understand where Saul went wrong and what God required. How can you more fully obey God today, based on what you learned from this chapter of Scripture?

How does the Holy Spirit impact your ability to obey and endure?

## DECIDE

When you're in a battle, decide to depend on the power of the Holy Spirit who enables you to endure and overcome.

# "God, What Do I Do When I Want to Give Up?"

### ▨ *Ehud: The Second Judge*

Then the Israelites cried out to the LORD, and he raised up Ehud son of Gera, a left-handed Benjaminite, as a deliverer for them. The Israelites sent him with the tribute for King Eglon of Moab.

JUDGES 3:15

## Read

JUDGES 3:12–23

Have you ever been tempted to quit something, even though you know you shouldn't? Maybe it's a healthy habit, a job, or a relationship? You might not be good at something *yet*, but that doesn't mean you never will be.

As I campaign for school board, there is a lot I don't know yet. There is still much to learn, and I need to be patient in the process. I'm also realizing that many of the skills God has developed in me over the years—public speaking, connecting with people, digital content creation—are useful in this endeavor too. God has been preparing me for something I never imagined doing.

How about you? Do you need some encouragement to hang in there and not give up? God can help us be responsible with what we've been entrusted with, one daily decision at a time, like he did with Ehud.

## Focus

In Judges 3:12, a familiar theme surfaces: "The Israelites again did what was evil in the LORD's sight." A Britney Spears song comes to mind, "Oops! . . . I Did It Again." But more than a catchy tune, the Israelites' anthem of disobedience hung over them like a banner of shame. God's people were supposed to think differently, act differently, even eat differently than the other nations. God had a specific purpose for them, and they fell short of that noble purpose. Maybe they thought it was restricting, too difficult, or impossible? Maybe they were ready to give up? Whatever the reason, they kept rebelling and suffered because of it.

At the end of Judges 3:12 we read that the Lord "gave King Eglon of Moab power over Israel, because they had done what was evil in the LORD's sight." In verses 13–14 we find out that the Ammonites and the Amalekites joined forces with King Eglon and attacked and defeated Israel. As a result of the battle, they took possession of the City of Palms, which was the ruins of Jericho. Then the Israelites served Eglon for eighteen years.

Daily decisions in the wrong direction can lead to years of preventable desperation. Daily decisions in the right direction can lead to years of peaceful satisfaction.

Life is hard. If we do the right thing, we are not guaranteed a life of ease. I know many followers of Jesus who have difficult lives and have been dealt some terrible blows. At the same time, there are those who do evil continually and seem to prosper. On this side of eternity, it is hard to make sense of it all, yet the Bible makes it clear that obeying God, whether in times of ease or great difficulty, is the right thing to do.

Don't give up. Ask the Holy Spirit to sustain you as you face challenges. You can experience peaceful satisfaction even in trying times when you faithfully follow the Lord. You may desire your circumstances to change, but deep within there is a sense of calm, knowing that God is in control.

## Engage

1. Look up at least three of the following verses and write them
   below, or summarize what you learn about who the Lord is
   through these verses.

**Faithful:** Hebrews 10:23

**Unchanging:** Malachi 3:6–7

**Loving:** 1 John 4:9

**Strong:** Isaiah 41:10

**A constant help in times of trouble:** Psalm 46:1

**Forgiving:** 1 John 1:9

**Unending:** Hebrews 7:22–25

By doing what they wanted, the Israelites were not only in opposition to God's loving and clear instructions but were subjected to oppression from King Eglon. Our focus verse today, Judges 3:15, talks about the Israelites crying out to God again for relief from their bondage. Sometimes people who rarely speak to God, or never have, will cry out to Him when they are suffering. When they do, God hears them. They are not alone. They are not forgotten. We see this time and time again throughout Scripture, including God hearing and responding to the cries of His people when they were in Egypt and when they were living under the oppression of the surrounding nations as recorded in Judges.

2. In response to the Israelites' pleas, and in His mercy, God raised up another judge and deliverer: Ehud. Reread Judges 3:15–17 and fill in the blanks below:

Ehud was the son of _____

He was a _____ - _____ Benjaminite.

Ehud made himself a _____ - _____

_____ that was _____ inches long.

He strapped it to his _____  _____

under his clothes.

Ehud brought the tribute to King Eglon of _____ ,

who was an extremely _____ man.

### Divine Assignment

This is the part where the kids in Sunday school start giggling, or at least wake up from their animal cracker and apple juice stupor, wide-eyed and eager to learn what happens next.

In Judges 3:18–23 we read the details of Ehud's covert military operation against King Eglon. It's a dramatic account. When Ehud is introduced, the text mentions he is left-handed. If you're a leftie, you know some things don't come easy in a predominately right-handed world. Yet lefties can have the upper hand (ha!) when it comes to things like sports or, in the case of Judges 3, a sneak attack against an evil ruler. (Don't try this at home, kids!)

Before we get into the nitty-gritty of this mission, it's worth noting that God created Ehud left-handed. It was no accident. All the days ordained for Ehud were written before one of them came to be (Ps. 139:16).

God knew He would give Ehud a divine assignment to defeat an oppressive ruler, and it would be possible for him to accomplish the task because the king would not suspect an assassin's blade to be on his right thigh, giving Ehud the advantage and leveraging the element of surprise. Reread the dramatic events of this account in Judges 3:18–23.

It's safe to assume that pride had infiltrated King Eglon's heart, and he likely underestimated Ehud. We don't know a lot about Ehud outside of this account in Judges 3, but it is evident he rose to the occasion and faithfully carried out his divine assignment with courage.

### Prime Real Estate

Have you ever wanted to see a different result in your life, but you knew the path to get there would be hard? Many people give up before they even try, or they cave partway through when the stakes are raised. Small daily decisions to do the right thing lead to lifelong faithfulness.

If you want to be found trustworthy to complete the sacred assignments God has entrusted to you, start with your thoughts. Your mind is prime real estate for what is built into your life. It is the foundation on which your decisions hinge.

What are you thinking about on a regular basis? Are you agreeing with lies or guarding against them? Are you wrangling wayward thoughts to the ground with the Word of God?

> Your mind is prime real estate for what is built into your life. It is the foundation on which your decisions hinge.

Ask the Holy Spirit to help you identify what is true and what is false, what is right and what is wrong, what is helpful and what is harmful. You can be disciplined in what you eat, how much sleep you get, and how often you move your body yet neglect to guard your thought life from sneak attacks or blatant onslaughts. It is important to practice faithful thoughts. Similar to getting your body in shape, renewing your mind is a daily exercise that directly impacts your actions. Training your mind to focus on what is true, noble, right, pure, lovely, admirable, excellent, and praiseworthy is a necessary and worthy pursuit (Phil. 4:8 NIV).

Here is an example:

*What is true?* Knowing God is still good even though my budget is stretched due to the increased price of gas and groceries.

*What is noble?* Going to God for help and wisdom instead of trying to figure it out on my own.

*What is right?* Reflecting on the ways God has provided in the past instead of rehearsing worry and anticipating worst-case scenarios.

*What is pure?* Believing God is my provider, like He says and proves in the Bible.

*What is lovely?* Receiving the help He offers instead of pridefully refusing to humble myself.

*What is admirable?* Evaluating where I can cut back and adjust.

*What is excellent?* Being generous with my time and talents instead of withholding what I can give.

*What is praiseworthy?* Thanking God for what I do have.

When we align our minds with God's truth, it informs our actions. On the other hand, letting our minds have a free-for-all and not wrangling rogue thoughts results in our feelings bossing us around, leaving us twisted up and confused. Faithful thoughts lead to courageous actions.

As the heat turns up and we get closer to Christ's return, I believe that courageous actions are needed more than ever before. Those actions could be pouring out your heart in prayer, sacrificing your resources to help others, speaking in front of a crowd that doesn't think like you do, standing up for truth even though it costs you greatly, and the list goes on. Whatever God calls you to, whether big or small, even if you are unsure what it is right now, you can be prepared to respond with courageous actions by daily exercising faithfulness to God in your thought life.

> Faithful thoughts lead to courageous actions.

Ehud completed the task set before him, even though it was intimidating and risky. God used him to accomplish His purposes. May we be faithful to God and not shrink back in difficult times. May it be said of us that we endured each day God ordained for us by relying on His strength, applying His wisdom, and carrying out His divine directives—even when we were intimidated and the stakes were high.

## Reflect

1. Read Hebrews 10:32–39. What are a key word, a phrase, and a sentence from this passage that stand out to you? Record them below.

   Word:

   Phrase:

   Sentence:

2. What is a divine assignment you have been given? How has God uniquely prepared or equipped you for this noble task?

## Bonus

Read Hebrews 13:20–21 as a benediction of blessing on this day of study. Write it below.

### DECIDE

When you want to give up, decide to strengthen your resolve to endure with faithful thoughts and courageous actions.

# "God, What Do I Do When I Experience Opposition?"

### ■ Ehud's Leadership

He told them, "Follow me, because the LORD has handed over your enemies, the Moabites, to you." So they followed him, captured the fords of the Jordan leading to Moab, and did not allow anyone to cross over.

JUDGES 3:28

## Read

JUDGES 3:24–30

Has God ever asked you to do something unconventional? Maybe it was making a career change, or giving away something of great value, or signing up to serve in a capacity that was out of your comfort zone. Or, in Ehud's case, carrying out a daring attack against an oppressive ruler. Or, in my case, running for local school board and trying to build bridges in a divisive time. There are people who oppose me who don't even know me. God has made it clear that I am to let Him defend me and not get caught in the weeds trying to defend myself. He is more than able to deal with the naysayers as I stay focused on the directives He has given.

In today's reading, we discover the dramatic conclusion of Ehud's attack on King Eglon and what he did next.

## Focus

God cares about the details—the places, the people, the words, and the actions. Judges 3:26 says Ehud "passed the Jordan near the carved images and reached Seirah." There is varying speculation among commentators about where this location was exactly, but both "carved images" and "Seirah" carry significance. They were landmarks that helped describe the specific route Ehud traveled.

As you follow God's lead during your time on earth, I'm sure there are physical landmarks that serve as signposts on your faith journey—maybe it is a house you lived in, a school you attended, a church where you served, or a business where you worked. Reflect on some crossroad moments—spiritual decisions—you have made that serve as spiritual mile markers along your faith journey. For example: "God led us to give away one of our vehicles to a friend who didn't have one. It grew our faith as we trusted His voice and depended on Him more."

## Engage

1. Summarize the key points from Judges 3:24–30 below:

   Verse 24:

Verse 25:

Verse 26:

Verse 27:

Verse 28:

Verse 29:

Verse 30:

Our church recently went through a series on biblical eldership. One of the key points throughout Scripture in selecting elders is that the elder should be Spirit-appointed (Acts 20:28), not self-appointed or chosen based on outward appearance (1 Sam. 16:7). Throughout the Bible, we see this principle applied as leaders were selected. In Judges 3:15, we read that the Lord lifted up Ehud as a deliverer for His people. After Ehud put King Eglon to death, he escaped to the hill country of Ephraim. Upon his arrival, as mentioned in verse 27, he sounded the ram's horn throughout the region. The Israelites came down with him from the hill country, and he became their leader.

King Eglon was dead, but there was more to be done to establish peace in the land. Ehud could not accomplish the task alone. Pay close attention to what he says to the people after that blast of the ram's horn rallied them: "Follow me, because the LORD has handed over your enemies, the Moabites, to you" (v. 28). Ehud's willingness to act and follow through in a high-stakes situation proved he was a capable leader, and the people accepted him as such. He incited them to follow him, not for his ego's sake but because the Lord was about to hand over their enemies to them. This seems to indicate the Lord revealed this coming victory to Ehud ahead of time, giving him a specific plan to carry out to accomplish His will.

The Israelites followed Ehud and captured the fords (the shallow places) of the Jordan River, which led to Moab, and they did not allow anyone to cross over. This reminds me of a scene from *The Fellowship of the Ring*. There is an epic battle between the demon Balrog and Gandalf the wizard on the Bridge of Khazad-dûm. Gandalf encourages those in his charge—the four hobbits, an elf, a dwarf, and two men—to cross over the bridge to safety. He goes last, a barrier between the evil aggressively pursuing them and the safety of the exit. As the demon prowls closer, Gandalf raises his staff and sword overhead, plants his feet firmly, and confronts him.

> "You cannot pass," he said. The orcs stood still, and a dead silence fell. "I am a servant of the Secret Fire, wielder of the flame of Anor. You cannot pass. The dark fire will not avail you, flame of Udûn. Go back to the Shadow! You cannot pass."[1]

It is interesting to note Gandalf faces off with darkness by courageously declaring his identity, exercising his given authority, speaking truth boldly, and holding his ground even when the earth beneath him begins to crumble. He stands in the gap between the vulnerable and the vexing, even though it may cost him everything. He is not willing to budge. Can the same be said of us?

When you encounter darkness:

- Courageously declare your identity (John 10:27–30).
- Exercise your God-given authority (Titus 2:11–15).
- Speak the truth boldly (2 Tim. 1:7).
- Hold your ground (Isa. 54:17).

When the Israelites rallied together, holding the line with Ehud, "they struck down about ten thousand Moabites, all stout and able-bodied men. Not one of them escaped" (Judg. 3:29). In unity they endured. They followed God's strategic plan, and He granted them success.

In verse 30 we read what happened because of their bravery and willingness to act and follow through: "Moab became subject to Israel that day, and the land had peace for eighty years." God's people experienced peace in the land for a significant amount of time. Eighty years. A lifetime for some. This peace was the fruit that came from their willingness to follow God's plan even when the opposition was fierce. They did not stop short of fulfilling His will. At last.

May the same be said of us.

## Reflect

1. Jot down some specific locations that have marked your faith walk.

2. What is one of your takeaways from the account of Ehud in Judges 3?

3. What is an area in your life where you are facing opposition? Talk to God about this situation, and ask Him to show you a Scripture you can cling to as you move forward. Second Chronicles 15:7 is solid ground to stand upon in a shaky world: "But as for you, be strong; don't give up, for your work has a reward."

**Bonus**

Ehud wasn't the only left-handed warrior in the Bible. Read the following verses and make a few notes about what you discover and the commonalities you find.

Judges 20:15–16

1 Chronicles 12:1–2

## DECIDE

When you experience opposition, decide to follow God's strategic lead as you endure.

# "God, What Do I Do Next?"

### ▓ *Shamgar: Son of Anath*

After Ehud, Shamgar son of Anath became judge. He also delivered Israel, striking down six hundred Philistines with a cattle prod.

JUDGES 3:31

## Read

JUDGES 3:31

Do you thrive on structure, or do you prefer a more open-ended approach to your day? Too many options can seem overwhelming, but not enough wiggle room can feel stifling. High school graduates often balk when asked, "What are you doing next?" It can be a daunting question. Whatever God has placed in front of you—however grand or ordinary, however complex or simple—tend to the next thing in front of you, with the wisdom and strength He supplies. It might be picking up a messy space, making an appointment, addressing a relational conflict, or weeding a garden. Whatever it is, ask God to help you see it through. When you focus on the end result, it can be too much. What if, instead, you focus on the next step, and then the one after that?

Today we're reading about Shamgar, who was tending to an ordinary task when suddenly God enabled him to do something extraordinary.

## Focus

Two sentences are the sum of today's Bible reading. However, a lot is said here. Judges 3:31 describes when Shamgar's brave act took place (after Ehud), who he was ("son of Anath" might refer to a person or a place), what he did (became a judge and delivered Israel), and how he helped deliver God's people (struck down six hundred Philistines with a cattle prod).

### What's in Your Hands?

Another term for cattle prod is a *goad*. John Schoenheit of Spirit & Truth explains,

> A goad is a 6-to-8-foot-long stick with a pointed end. This instrument was used by farmers to train their oxen to move in a straight line. The goad poked the shoulder, not hurting the animal, but showing them the way. When Scripture says "The words of the Lord are like goads," it means they make us wise by guiding us and keeping us moving in the right direction.[1]

The goad was to the farmer like the staff was to the shepherd: an effective tool to train and protect stubborn animals, keeping them from danger and from wandering off.

Shamgar used what he had available to accomplish the divine directive he'd been given: a cattle prod. It was unconventional but effective. It's possible he was a farmer and used what he had on hand, or literally in his hand, to carry out this courageous feat. This example supports what we see throughout Scripture: God supernaturally accomplishes His purposes through willing, ordinary, and imperfect people with great faith.

> God supernaturally accomplishes His purposes through willing, ordinary, and imperfect people with great faith.

Consider this observation from Matthew Henry regarding Shamgar:

It is probable he was himself following the plough when the Philistines made an inroad upon the country to ravage it, and God put it into his heart to oppose them; the impulse being sudden and strong, and having neither sword nor spear to do execution with, he took the instrument that was next at hand, some of the tools of this plough, and with that killed so many hundred men and came off unhurt. God can make those eminently serviceable to his glory and his church's good whose extraction, education, and employment, are very mean and obscure. He that has the residue of the Spirit could, when he pleased, make ploughmen judges and generals, and fishermen apostles. It is no matter how weak the weapon is if God direct and strengthen the arm. An ox-goad, when God pleases, shall do more than Goliath's sword. And sometimes he chooses to work by such unlikely means, that the excellency of the power may appear to be of God.[2]

God used Joseph to provide for His people in famine (Gen. 47:13–27).

God used Moses to deliver His people from Pharaoh's oppressive rule (Exod. 3).

God used Rahab to hide the two Israelite spies in Jericho (Josh. 2).

God used the judges to deliver the Israelites from the surrounding nations (Judg. 1–5).

God used Ruth to birth Obed, the grandfather of King David, and be part of the lineage of Christ (Ruth 4:13–22).

God used David to rule and reign as king over His people (2 Sam. 5:1–5).

God used Esther to save the Israelites from destruction (Esther 7).

Looking over this small sampling of leaders, we could use labels like *arrogant, insecure, murderer, prostitute, outsider, adulterer,* or *victim.* Or we could use labels like *refined, chosen, brave, willing, faithful, redeemed, forgiven,* or *defender.* Each of these people had limitations, yet God called them to something greater than themselves and equipped them to do the things He had prepared ahead of time for them to do.

### Small Things

Often we focus on big things, like the above biblical events, as incredible acts of faith. But our daily, ordinary tasks can be done with great faith too. We learn to endure day by day as we care for those God has entrusted to us while in the place, position, and divine directives He has given us. As we learn to rely on Jesus to get us through the small things, we will be strengthened for the bigger things to come.

My hunch is that Shamgar's faith developed incrementally over time. We only have a snapshot of his life, one recorded moment of heroic proportions, preserved in the canon of Scripture.

How are you using what God has placed in your hands?

You might not be striking down the enemy with farming equipment, but you may be teaching young children to use the Word of God to defeat the enemy. Or you may be treating your coworker with kindness even though they have treated you unfairly. Or you may be sacrificially investing in a nonprofit that is restoring dignity to broken people. Whatever God has asked you to do, don't bail when it is hard. What if breakthrough is right around the corner, or what if the day-in, day-out hard work is preparing you for your "Shamgar" moment, when God asks you to bravely act even when it looks like the odds are stacked against you?

No matter what you are facing, God is the firm foundation that holds when you are shaken. He is the One who enables you to endure.

## Engage

1. Read Psalm 18:27–40 and ask the Holy Spirit to highlight a few verses. Record them below:

2. With God's help, you can endure until the end and finish well. As we conclude today's study, take some time to read Revelation 2:1–7 and record what you learn about endurance:

3. Write out Revelation 2:3 below:

4. Read Revelation 14:6–13 and write out verse 12:

### Reflect

Is there something God lovingly wants to confront and address and deliver you from? Ask Him about it. Ask Him to show you specific Scripture to instruct you in this matter.

**Bonus**

Take some time to work on memorizing the key verse from this week of study:

And let endurance have its full effect, so that you may be mature and complete, lacking nothing. (James 1:4)

---

### DECIDE

When you don't know what to do next, decide to endure in the cause of Christ as you carry out your daily tasks.

---

*Dear Jesus,*

*You are the perfect example of endurance to us. You endured the cross on our behalf. You did not give up. We are weak, but in You and through You and because of You we can be strong. Help us to faithfully carry out our daily tasks in ways that honor You. May we not give way to fear but willingly follow through with Your divine directives for us. It's tempting to be discouraged and to doubt Your goodness when we face difficulties, but You are good. You keep Your promises, and You will not abandon us!*

*Thank You for Your mercy that covers us, Your care that surrounds us, Your armor that shields us. We are not left to fend for ourselves in this battle. You have equipped us to stand. You have gone ahead of us. You are victorious. We don't always understand Your ways, but we know Your thoughts are higher than our thoughts, and Your ways are better than our ways. Amen.*

# WEEK 3 WRAP-UP

*This week, I decide to endure through the power of the Holy Spirit and the armor of God.*

Answer the following questions to help summarize what you learned during this week of study. If possible, use biblical references to back up your responses.

1. What weapon of warfare will you utilize today (God's Word, prayer, worship, Jesus's name, your testimony, fasting, thanksgiving)?

2. How does the Bible define *endurance*, based on the Scriptures you read this week?

3. How did Othniel, Ehud, and Shamgar demonstrate endurance, as recorded in Judges?

4. What is one example of Jesus demonstrating endurance during His time on earth?

5. Based on what you discovered in Lessons 1–5, how can the decision to endure help you make wise decisions in uncertain times?

# THE DECISION TO RISE

## JUDGES 4

Now that we understand what it means to endure as we follow Christ throughout this life, it's time to dig into Judges 4. This week of study will focus on the account of Deborah and Barak and how they worked together to lead God's people during a tumultuous time. You will discover that the decision to faithfully rise to your God-given position and follow His lead is what is needed to navigate the difficulties of life with wisdom.

Rise up; this matter is in your hands. We will support you, so take courage and do it. (NIV)

# LESSON 1

## "God, What Do I Do When I'm Worried?"

### ▨ *Deborah: Prophetess and Judge*

Deborah, a prophetess and the wife of Lappidoth, was judging Israel at that time.

JUDGES 4:4

**Read**

JUDGES 4:1–5

Behaving badly is often a by-product of forgotten identity. Or it can be a result of finding our identity in temporal things instead of eternal things. I used to be a worrier—making lists of what I did not have, imagining worst-case scenarios, feeling the stress of trying to figure it all out. But God set me free from all of that. I am not a worrier anymore. I no longer identify as a wound-up woman. Yet the other day, when faced with challenging circumstances, I briefly gave in to the spin cycle again. I reverted to someone I no longer am: I was doubting, anxious, and trying to solve problems through a flurry of worry that left me feeling defeated and short-tempered.

We are all a work in progress. We lose sight of what is most true when we operate out of doubt and fear, fixing our eyes on the craziness of the world and reacting to what we see with our natural eyes instead of operating by faith, setting our mind on things above, and standing on the promises of God. But we are of another kingdom. One where Christ is already victorious!

Although not a lot is written about Deborah, we clearly see that she operated from a place of godly confidence amid worrisome situations.

## Focus

In Judges 4:3, we encounter the iron chariots again. Sisera, Jabin's commander, had nine hundred of them! Talk about a troubling situation. These chariot armies would have been highly trained, maybe like the Navy SEALs or Marines of our day. As one commentator says, "Chariot horses were specifically bred and trained for combat. Most horses will not voluntarily proceed into the kinds of situations pictured on monuments. They must be trained to charge, trample, and obey commands under noisy, frightening circumstances."[1]

In response to this threat, we read about how the Israelites cried out to the Lord for relief from their oppression (Judg. 4:3). God's people knew He was in charge, and even though they strayed or forgot at times, they remembered to go to Him when they were suffering. They knew God could turn things around.

It is admirable to go to the Lord for help, and not just when the "iron chariots" press in. The goal is to always remember Him, in the good and bad, and to follow His loving instructions, not to call out to Him only when we get caught in our sin or are trying to minimize or escape negative consequences. Yet it's better to run to Him in trouble than not at all. Jesus stands ready to receive us, with nail-scarred hands, whenever we humbly return to Him in repentance. He can't wait to restore us. It is good and right to seek Him, not simply for a blessing but because He is worthy and we are created for this purpose: a close, personal relationship with God.

When I was having my worry fest the other night, God prompted me to tell Him about the worries in prayer. So I listed them to Him instead of keeping them trapped on the hamster wheel in my mind. Acknowledging the burdens helped me release them to Him, transferring the weight off my shoulders and onto His.

Speaking on situations ripe for worry, what if God asked you to lead a vast group of people, morally and militarily, and no one like you had ever had the position before? It could be tempting to avoid the calling out of fear, instead of willingly rising to the task, full of faith. Yet, in the following verse we see how Deborah, the next judge, responded. Judges 4:4 says, "Deborah, a prophetess and the wife of Lappidoth, was judging Israel at that time."

Deborah arose as "a mother in Israel" (5:7). While we don't know for sure if Deborah was a literal mother of biological children or if this phrase referred to her role of overseeing the Israelites, it remains clear that she was available and willing to care for those God had entrusted to her.

The name Deborah means "bee."[2] Let's pause and think about honeybees for a moment. The worker bees daily produce what is needed for their hive. They are willing to sacrifice themselves when threatened. They pollinate plants and make honey, which benefits their immediate colony and the entire ecosystem. Their efforts are multiplied, and they impact many beyond their immediate sphere of influence. The same can be said of Deborah. She rose to the occasion to provide what was needed. She was willing to sacrifice, act courageously, bypass the naysayers, and work for God and the good of His people. Her faith left a legacy for us to learn from. Like the other judges we read about, Deborah's willingness to rise and serve as a temporary deliverer foreshadowed the greater need for a complete and permanent Deliverer: Jesus.

## Engage

1. Write down a summary of the following verses, or choose one or two verses from each passage to write down, especially as it relates to faith.

   2 Corinthians 4:16–18

Hebrews 11:1–6

When we see only with our natural eyes, we miss the mark. We get tripped up in the tedious, we bypass the blessings, we rehearse the lack.

2. Reread Judges 4:1–2 to see what happened when God's people forgot who He was and who they were in Him. Summarize each verse below:

Verse 1:

Verse 2:

3. Read Joshua 11:1–11 in order to get the backstory about Israel's previous relationship with Jabin, king of Hazor. What was the result of the conquest?

4. According to Isaiah 31:1, what is a wise move for those who find themselves in intimidating situations?

### Learning from History

Various commentators note that the city of Hazor, referred to in Judges 4:2, must have been rebuilt after being destroyed, and perhaps this Jabin was an ancestor of the Jabin whom Joshua and the army dealt with in Joshua 11. Some others note that Jabin could have been a title, like Pharaoh, Czar, or Caesar.[3]

The oppression the Israelites experienced from Jabin was especially difficult because their ancestors had already gained victory from Hazor. Matthew Henry's commentary about this ancient situation mirrors our present reality: "To be oppressed by those whom their fathers had conquered, and whom they themselves had foolishly spared, could not but be very grievous."[4] May we learn from their mistakes and do better. May we not give up the ground of liberation that our ancestors fought so hard to give us. May we not mock their sacrifice with our apathy or compromise or disregard their costly battles. May we not willingly walk back into the bondage our ancestors worked so hard to free us from. May our generation fight to gain holy ground for our children and grandchildren and not be silent observers in their demise.

### *Prophetesses in Scripture*

Deborah was a prophetess and judge. This is an interesting combination. Throughout Scripture, we learn about other prophetesses and what they did. Read each passage and record the main points. Underneath the verses, include a few summary sentences and then write out a simple prayer based on what you learned from Scripture. This will take some time, but it will be worth it as you dig into Scripture for yourself and learn more about these fascinating women. The first one is done for you.

**Name of Prophetess: Miriam**
**Bible Verse(s) | Bio | Info | Actions**

> Exodus 15:19–21: Miriam was the sister of Moses and Aaron; she led women in worship with instruments and dancing after God parted the Red Sea and their enemies were destroyed.
>
> Numbers 12:1–15: Miriam and Aaron sinned by speaking out against Moses; God punished Miriam with leprosy for seven days.
>
> Numbers 20:1; 26:59: Miriam died and was buried in the Desert of Zin, at Kadesh. Miriam's father was Amram and her mother was Jochebed, a descendant of Levi.
>
> Micah 6:4: God reminded His people how He redeemed them from slavery in Egypt and how He sent Moses to lead them, as well as Aaron and Miriam.

**Summary:**
Miriam was a prophet and leader. She led the women in worship after they crossed the Red Sea. She sinned due to her envy of Moses and experienced serious consequences for her actions because of it.

**Prayer:**
*God, help me to use my influence for good and rest secure in the position You have chosen for me.*

**Name of Prophetess: D**_____

    Judges 4:4–5:15:

**Summary:**

**Prayer:**

**Name of Prophetess: H**_____

2 Kings 22:14:

2 Chronicles 34:22:

**Summary:**

**Prayer:**

**Name of Prophetess: N**_____

Nehemiah 6:14:

**Summary:**

**Prayer:**

**Name of Prophetess: Wife of** _____

Isaiah 8:3:

**Summary:**

**Prayer:**

**Name of Prophetess: A**_____

Luke 2:36–38:

**Summary:**

**Prayer:**

**Name of Prophetess: four** _____ **of** _____

Acts 21:8–9:

**Summary:**

**Prayer:**

**Name of Prophetess: J**‗‗‗‗‗‗‗‗‗‗‗‗‗‗‗‗‗‗‗‗‗‗‗‗

Revelation 2:20:

**Summary:**

**Prayer:**

## Reflect

1. There are two false prophetesses mentioned in the previous activity; who were they and what were their wrongdoings?

2. According to what you read in Judges 4:4–5:15, how is Deborah similar to some of the prophetesses listed above, and how is she different?

### *At That Time*

Judges 4:4 ends, "Deborah was judging Israel at that time." *At that time.* It's no mistake Deborah lived when she did. And it's no mistake YOU are living now, at *this* time.

God is outside of time, yet, for now, we humans live within time frames and boundary lines and specific coordinates (Acts 17:26–27). Sometimes we bemoan the times we are living in, but it is intentional, on purpose. When faced with situations out of our comfort zone that stretch our abilities, we are positioned to feel our dependence on the Lord. That dependence is always there, yet we really feel it when we are tasked with sacred assignments that look giant-sized to the natural eye.

Being called to judge Israel was a giant-sized task. These were a stubborn and rebellious people whom God loved and chose, yet they kept forgetting their true identity. They continually operated out of doubt and fear, rehearsing their lack instead of focusing on the milk and honey—the abundance God had given them. They had been set free, yet they seemed to prefer their chains—until it became too much and they cried out for deliverance.

### Under the Palm

Judges 4:5 says, "[Deborah] would sit under the palm tree of Deborah between Ramah and Bethel in the hill country of Ephraim, and the Israelites went up to her to settle disputes." Her location for settling the disputes of God's people was under a particular palm tree. I like to think this is symbolic of Deborah sitting under the palm of God's hand, willingly situated under the oversight and covering of the One she worshiped and from whom she gained wisdom.

Where you are positioned matters—from a physical and spiritual standpoint. It is no mistake you are living at this time in history, in a specific zip code, at a particular street address. No matter your occupation or social status, you can influence others in a way that honors God as you interact with the people around you and carry out the specific tasks He has given you.

What a noble and necessary calling we have: to leave a legacy of belief in Jesus for the generations coming after us.

> What a noble and necessary calling we have: to leave a legacy of belief in Jesus for the generations coming after us.

Like Deborah, may we rise to obey God and complete the tasks He has entrusted to us, even when there is great risk. Like Miriam, may we lead others in celebrating the miraculous deliverance God has provided for His people. Like Huldah, may we believe God's Word and communicate it clearly to others. Like Anna in her old age, may we be found, in this very hour, giving thanks to God and speaking of Jesus to all who have not yet received His redemption for their sins (Luke 2:38).

**Bonus**

What have you been worried about lately? Take some time and talk to God about these worries, then heave them upon His strong, capable shoulders. Trust Him with the results. Write out a prayer of release below:

## DECIDE

When you are worried, decide to rise
with faith and leave a legacy of belief.

# "God, What Do I Do When I'm Intimidated?"

### ■ *Barak: Son of Abinoam*

Barak said to her, "If you will go with me, I will go. But if you will not go with me, I will not go."

JUDGES 4:8

**Read**

JUDGES 4:6–10

When we feel intimidated, we might shrink back faster than a cat from a spraying hose. Or we may approach intimidation like a peacock, strutting our stuff in an effort to one-up the competition. Regardless of our reflexive response—to shrink back or steamroll when intimidated—it is important that we don't take our marching orders from our emotions but listen carefully to God's instructions for our next steps, like Barak did.

## Focus

We have arrived at the buildup to an epic battle. This is where the haunting melody swells as Deborah rises to carry out one of her most important tasks as prophetess and judge. We see this in Judges 4:6–7, which says,

> [Deborah] summoned Barak son of Abinoam from Kedesh in Naphtali and said to him, "Hasn't the Lord, the God of Israel, commanded you, 'Go, deploy the troops on Mount Tabor, and take with you ten thousand men from the Naphtalites and Zebulunites? Then I will lure Sisera commander of Jabin's army, his chariots, and his infantry at the Wadi Kishon to fight against you, and I will hand him over to you.'"

## Engage

1. Barak is mentioned in two other places in Scripture. Read these verses, then jot down a key piece of information you want to remember about him from each passage.

   1 Samuel 12:6–11:

   Hebrews 11:32–34:

2. Fill in the missing word below based on Hebrews 11:32–34. Then underline the verbs (action words) from the list. The first verb is done for you.

By _____ Gideon, Barak, Samson, Jephthah, David, Samuel, and the prophets:

- <u>Conquered</u> kingdoms
- Administered justice
- Obtained promises
- Shut the mouths of lions
- Quenched the raging of fire
- Escaped the edge of the sword
- Gained strength in weakness
- Became mighty in battle
- Put foreign armies to flight

### By Faith

Sometimes we put more focus on what has been done and not enough focus on how it was done. Hebrews 11 is often called "the faith chapter" or "the Hall of Faith." Many of those mentioned in this chapter were very flawed people whom God used in amazing ways because of the common denominator of faith. The reason they could do the things listed above is because they believed that God could do the impossible. They did not shrink back, and their faith still inspires us today. According to Matthew 17:20, it only takes a mustard seed of faith to move a mountain. Isn't that encouraging? *Oh, God, increase our faith!*

Have you ever had a friend remind you of truth you had forgotten, were unsure about, or had overlooked? Have you been that kind of friend to someone else? When Deborah summoned Barak, it appears she was either reminding him of what he had been commanded to do by God or she was informing him of what God had made clear to her regarding him: "Hasn't the Lord, the God of Israel, commanded you, 'Go, deploy the troops on Mount Tabor, and take with you ten thousand men from the Naphtalites and Zebulunites?'" (Judg. 4:6).

According to the article "What Does Scripture Teach About the Office of Prophet and Gift of Prophecy" by pastor Sam Storms,

A prophet's primary function in the Old Testament was to serve as God's representative or ambassador by communicating God's word to his people.

True prophets never spoke on their own authority or shared their personal opinions, but rather delivered the message God himself gave them.[1]

The apostle Peter helps define prophecy: "Above all, you know this: No prophecy of Scripture comes from the prophet's own interpretation, because no prophecy ever came by the will of man; instead, men spoke from God as they were carried along by the Holy Spirit" (2 Pet. 1:20–21).

Deborah as prophetess and judge was reiterating to Barak what God revealed to her. She was His mouthpiece to Barak.

### Following God's Instructions

Deborah was not the only person in Scripture to exhort someone to carry out God's instructions. Read each passage, then record your answers to the following questions (the first example is completed for you):

- Who instructed or exhorted the main character?
- What were the instructions, declaration, or exhortation they gave?
- Did the person follow through in carrying out the instructions they were given? (You may have to read a little bit more to uncover this answer.)

**Genesis 12:1–8**

Who: God instructed Abram.

What: God told him to go to the land He would show him. God promised Abram He would make him into a great nation and bless him, that all the peoples of the earth would be blessed through him.

Did they rise to the occasion? Yes, in verse 4, it says that Abram "went, as the Lord had told him."

**Ruth 1:1–5, 11–17**

Who:

What:

Did they rise to the occasion?

**1 Samuel 3:1–21**

Who:

What:

Did they rise to the occasion?

**Esther 4:1–17**

Who:

What:

Did they rise to the occasion?

**Isaiah 6:1–9**

Who:

What:

Did they rise to the occasion?

### The Jezreel Valley

Barak was commanded by God to deploy the troops on Mount Tabor. This location is significant and unique. Dr. Leonard, our guide on my trip to the Holy Land, pointed out Mount Tabor when we were near Nazareth, on top of Mount Precipice. Its symmetrical mound shape makes it easy to spot. It is not extremely tall—1,886 feet high—but it rises above the lowland of the most fertile valley in the land: the Jezreel Valley. This valley region is the "honey" section of Israel—a place of vast farmland and abundance—the fulfillment of the promise God gave His people in the time of Moses. Exodus 3:7–8 reminds us of this promise:

> Then the LORD said, "I have observed the misery of my people in Egypt, and have heard them crying out because of their oppressors. I know about their sufferings, and I have come down to rescue them from the power of the Egyptians and to bring them from that land to a good and spacious land, a land flowing with milk and honey—the territory of the Canaanites, Hethites, Amorites, Perizzites, Hivites, and Jebusites."

Mount Precipice is the midway point between Megiddo and Mount Tabor. Across the valley is Mount Gilboa. *The Moody Bible Commentary*

states, "Mount Tabor is the primary landmark along the international trade route in this region. The gathering of a major military force at Mount Tabor had obvious military significance to those who need to keep the trade route open."[2] This is the landscape for the pending battle in Judges 4.

We know from verse 3 that Sisera, the commander of Jabin's army, cruelly oppressed the Israelites. The coming battle is a result of two decades of captivity under the iron chariots and iron fist of Sisera. In verse 7, Deborah reveals God's military strategy to Barak and even what the result will be: "Then I will lure Sisera commander of Jabin's army, his chariots, and his infantry at the Wadi Kishon to fight against you, and I will hand him over to you." This wadi was "a swampy area near Megiddo" that was wide enough for Jabin's army, his chariots and infantry, to navigate; however, Wadi Kishon can "turn into a quagmire in the rain."[3]

It's reassuring to know the outcome of the battle before entering it. But I imagine that God's command to Barak to engage in an attack against Sisera was still unsettling, given the strength of Sisera's army and the force with which they had oppressed the Israelites for years. The enemy was intimidating, but the directives were clear.

Deborah followed through on God's instructions to her and, in turn, Barak followed through on his. Your willingness to obey God can help challenge, sharpen, and empower others to do the same. When you decide to obey God, it has a ripple effect in the lives of those around you. The same can be said when we disobey God: the effects of sin can ripple into the lives of others. We have seen many examples of the latter throughout our study of Judges, so let's focus on the successful example before us; it's refreshing.

In Judges 4:8, Barak says to Deborah, "If you will go *with me*, I will go. But if you will not go *with me*, I will not go" (emphasis added). Why do you think Barak responded in this way? Was he afraid? Did he want Deborah to go because he respected her insight and role? Or was it something else?

Deborah favorably responded to Barak's request to accompany him in battle. She also made the following clear to Barak: "You will receive no honor on the road you are about to take, because the LORD will sell Sisera to a woman" (v. 9). The woman mentioned here is not Deborah but Jael, whom we will get to know in coming lessons.

Next, we read, "Deborah got up and went with Barak to Kedesh. Barak summoned Zebulun and Naphtali to Kedesh; ten thousand men followed him, and Deborah also went with him" (vv. 9–10). Deborah's obedience to God influenced Barak's obedience to God, which influenced ten thousand men to follow Barak into battle. Courage is contagious.

> Courage is contagious.

## Reflect

1. Has God asked you to accompany someone into a battle they were facing? In what specific ways were you there for them?

2. Who has accompanied you into a battle, either in the past or currently? In what ways did they help you be brave and follow through?

*Dear God, help me operate by faith, believing You fulfill Your promises. Thank You for the example of others who have stepped up to obey You instead of shrinking back. I want to speak what is true and fear You more than what others think of me. By Your strength and grace, may my life of obedience inspire others to wholeheartedly follow You. In Jesus's name, Amen.*

**Bonus**

Read John 8:28–30 and 12:49–50 and record what you learn about Jesus being a mouthpiece for God.

## DECIDE

When you feel intimidated, decide to rise up instead of shrinking back, and others will do the same.

## LESSON 3

# "God, What Do I Do When I Feel Alone?"

### ▓ *Deborah and Barak in Battle*

Then Deborah said to Barak, "Go! This is the day the LORD has handed Sisera over to you. Hasn't the LORD gone before you?"

JUDGES 4:14

### Read

JUDGES 4:11–16

I have experienced my share of loneliness, some circumstantial, some self-inflicted, yet God has used this pain to develop empathy and compassion in me. He is able to help us lead our loneliness instead of letting it boss us around. Sometimes the very loneliness we are feeling can be a catalyst to reach out to others so they don't have to experience similar pain. The enemy likes to isolate us from one another so he can more easily attack. Let's be aware of his schemes!

God created us for community and connection, and whether we are extroverted or introverted, married or single, old or young, we are designed for companionship.

It really is true that we are better together. Many of us are settling for a counterfeit version of connection and missing out on the joys and refining growth that come through in-person interactions. Our strengths can be maximized and our weaknesses can be minimized when we live in healthy community. Healthy community does not mean flawless, nor does it mean our feelings will never get hurt. When we do life together instead of operating as islands, we are positioned to flourish in ways we never could have in isolation. Barak and Deborah are great examples of collaborating instead of battling alone.

> God created us for community and connection, and whether we are extroverted or introverted, married or single, old or young, we are designed for companionship.

## Focus

In Judges 4:11, we again read about Moses's father-in-law. This verse specifically mentions that Heber the Kenite moved away from the Kenites and pitched his tent beside the oak tree of Zaanannim, near Kedesh. This fact will soon come into play.

In verse 12 we learn that it was reported to Sisera that Barak had gone up Mount Tabor, and verse 13 reveals Sisera responded to Barak's action by summoning all nine hundred of his iron chariots and all the troops who were with him, from Harosheth of the Nations to the Wadi Kishon. It is likely that Barak's ten thousand troops were on foot and ripe for attack from the power of the charging iron chariots. In the natural realm, the odds were stacked against the Israelites, yet Deborah reminds Barak of God's command and the promised result He had made known: "Then Deborah said to Barak, 'Go! This is the day the LORD has handed Sisera over to you. Hasn't the LORD gone before you?' So Barak came down from Mount Tabor with ten thousand men following him" (v. 14).

Sometimes we need to be reminded about what God has already said and what He has already done, for and through those who have gone before us. Sometimes we need to borrow courage from those beside us.

I admire the collaborative leadership of Deborah and Barak. She was not a one-woman show, and he was not a one-man show. They were both leaders called by God to accomplish specific purposes during the times in which they lived. They linked arms instead of facing off; they offered their God-given strengths and unique giftings for His glory and the greater good, not for individual fame or notoriety. They yielded to one another's abilities without discounting their own. They did not steamroll, nor did they shrink back. They doubled their strength instead of dividing it. They complemented one another for the sake of the kingdom.

Under God's divine leadership and practical directives, Barak and Deborah were unstoppable. They each fulfilled their assigned role, leading God's people into battle and to promised victory. It was a faith-infused partnership. They cooperated with God, and He provided the success. They did their part and trusted Him to do what He said He would do.

In verse 15 we read, "The LORD threw Sisera, all his charioteers, and all his army into a panic before Barak's assault. Sisera left his chariot and fled on foot."

It can look like the odds are against you, the scales are unbalanced, and you are outnumbered and outwitted with no clear path to victory. *But God!* He can take your willingness, your mustard seed faith, your little bit of courage, and mix it with His matchless power and do the impossible—jaw-dropping, wide-eyed wonders that have no explanation apart from Him. Sometimes they take place in the Jezreel Valley, and other times they happen in the midst of ordinary moments, without a lot of fanfare or hype.

## Engage

1. Read the following passages and record what you learn about God's presence.

   Deuteronomy 31:5–6

Isaiah 45:1–2

Isaiah 52:12

Isaiah 58:8

Galatians 2:20–21

Ezekiel 36:24–28

These Scriptures show us that the Lord goes ahead of His people (as a forerunner), goes behind us (as a rear guard), is with us (Emmanuel), and is within us (Holy Spirit). Even when you feel alone, if you believe in Christ, you are hemmed in, shielded, and have a faithful companion who will not let you down or forsake you. You are surrounded in the best possible way!

## Reflect

1. Is there an area in your life where you are steamrolling others instead of making room for their leadership? If so, why do you think this is your tendency?

2. Is there an area in your life where you are shrinking back instead of offering the strength and unique gifting God has given you? If so, why do you think this is your tendency?

3. Have you witnessed a miracle, or have you heard about a miracle from an eyewitness? What happened, and how did this miracle increase your faith?

### No Turning Back

Barak fulfilled what God asked of him through faith in Him *and* through action (Heb. 11:6; James 2:26). But it seems Barak's actions were also spurred on by Deborah's faith in God, her exhortation for him to attack Sisera's army, and the assurance she'd heard from God. Let's not overlook the willingness of the ten thousand brave men who followed Barak as they confronted the enemy. Barak, Deborah, and these troops all played vital roles in this attack.

Some of you may need to hear this loud and clear: You may not receive the accolades that out-front leaders do, but that does not minimize or negate the vital role *you* play in the victory of "your people"—your family, friends, church, coworkers, and community. Interceding grandparents, parents, aunts, uncles, and mentors all over the world have impacted generations with the gospel. We may not know their names or see the magnitude of the spiritual ground they gain as they war in prayer, but God knows. He knew the name of every man in the troop of ten thousand who marched forward. He knows you. You are not overlooked in the kingdom. Being willing to go into battle alongside a godly, faith-filled leader who is getting their marching orders from God is no small thing. Being willing to stand for truth even when no one else will might be necessary now and in the coming days. But it is better to do it together whenever possible. It is wise to rise with others instead of alone. But if "none go with me, still I will follow. No turning back, no turning back."[1]

### Follow Through in Faith

The last verse in today's study is Judges 4:16. "Barak pursued the chariots and the army as far as Harosheth of the Nations, and the whole army of Sisera fell by the sword; not a single man was left." At last! Here is someone who carried out God's instructions completely. Barak did not partially obey; he followed through and he finished well. He may have been hesitant at first, but in the end he was faithful to complete the work he had been charged with by almighty God. His success is attributed to his faith and the availability and faithfulness of those around him—Deborah and the troops.

As I campaign for school board, I have a small yet mighty army around me, providing prayer support, manpower, exhortation, and resources needed to face the "iron chariots" along the way. There are some things only I can do and other things I am relying on others to do. The point is, when we each step up to do our part, collaborating for a purpose greater than ourselves, the mission is accomplished with God's help.

It's your turn, my friend. Go! This is the day the Lord has made, and He goes before you, behind you, and with you, and He dwells within you. Whether you are out front or behind the scenes, whether you have a big or small task, whether you stand alone or with others, ask God to reveal your marching orders, then move forward in faith and joy, assured of His mighty and loving presence.

Through Jesus, and your faith in Him, there is nothing that will separate you from God's love. You are never alone when you belong to Christ, no matter what battle you are facing or will face in the future. Take shelter under His wings as you go forth—borrow His courage, follow His voice, and take ground for the kingdom.

## Bonus

Draw a picture of what God's presence looks like and feels like to you. Does it look like a cozy blanket, an impenetrable shield, downy soft wings, a fortified tower of refuge, or something else?

## DECIDE

When you feel alone, decide to be
wise and rise with others.

# LESSON 4

# "God, What Do I Do When I'm Bombarded by Lies?"

### *Jael and the Tent Peg*

When Barak arrived in pursuit of Sisera, Jael went out to greet him and said to him, "Come and I will show you the man you are looking for." So he went in with her, and there was Sisera lying dead with a tent peg through his temple!

JUDGES 4:22

## Read

JUDGES 4:17–23

Whether it comes from media outlets, a class textbook, an "expert," or the person in the mirror, we are bombarded by lies daily. The more we listen, the more we don't combat the lie with the truth. The more we start to believe falsehood and live it out, the more stuck we become. Thankfully, Jesus is the way, the truth, and the life, and He can expose lies we have believed and deliver us into freedom through the truth of His Word. The truth sets us free, indeed! It is my prayer that during today's lesson, God would show each of us how to take action, using His effective measures, to combat the lies that bombard our minds.

## Focus

There is a shirt I wear and sell at speaking events and on my website, from the company Elly & Grace. I call it my Power Squad shirt. I've included what it says below. This list highlights a faith action taken by each of these women from Scripture. This sisterhood of imperfect yet courageous women inspires me to serve God in big and small ways.

Circle one action from the list that you want to get better at. Ask God to grow that quality in you. For example, I chose "prayed." I want prayer to be my first to-do when I am faced with troubling situations.

**RUTH** LOVED.

**DEBORAH** LED.

**MIRIAM** DANCED.

**MARY** BELIEVED.

**ESTHER** SACRIFICED.

**MARTHA** SERVED.

**HANNAH** PRAYED.

**NAOMI** OVERCAME.

**JAEL** FOUGHT.

### Jaelle the Brave

Speaking of Jael, I know a Jaelle in real life. She's thirteen. She's fought with courage that came from God Himself. No, she didn't drive a tent peg through Sisera's temple. But through her faith and bravery, along with that of her parents and a community that provided prayer support, practical help, and medical intervention, young Jaelle drove a tent peg through the enemy's plans to take her out.

Jaelle was in kidney failure at age ten. Her blood pressure was at a dangerous level, and her heart was taxed from working overtime. Throughout this unexpected and difficult journey Jaelle reminded her parents "God is working; we just need to wait." After months of dialysis, tears, and delays, she had a kidney transplant that saved her life. Her dad was a perfect match! But before the transplant happened, her dad's life was spared because doctors detected a heart issue when he underwent the vigorous testing required for the transplant process. This issue would not have been revealed otherwise. Once he had recovered from his procedure, the kidney transplant took place. Jaelle's dad offered the part of himself that was needed to give her new life.

What an awe-inspiring picture of the gospel! Father God freely offered Jesus to save you from destruction—from the disease of sin and the despair of death. Jesus sacrificed Himself completely, out of His great love for you. If you choose to accept this lavish gift of salvation, you can be born again and made new—a necessary heart transplant (Ezek. 36:26–27).

Young Jaelle is a living testimony of God's goodness and ability to work and heal against earthly odds. Her story has strengthened the faith of many and will continue to do so.[1]

### Jael from the Bible

Let's take a look at biblical Jael, whom she fought against, and how she fought. In Judges 4:17, we discover that Sisera, commander of Jabin's army, fled on foot to Jael's tent. Jael was the wife of Heber the Kenite, who was mentioned in verse 11. Sisera sought refuge at this couple's tent because there was peace between King Jabin of Hazor and Heber's family.

In verse 18, Jael greets Sisera, invites him into her tent, and tells him not to be afraid. In the Eastern world, hospitality is ingrained in the culture. Friends, strangers, and even enemies can find respite within the walls of this ancient practice. It is commonplace to make sure the needs of guests are taken care of, that they are comfortable and have food to eat and a place to rest.

Let's reread verses 18–19: "So he went into her tent, and she covered him with a blanket. He said to her, 'Please give me a little water to drink for I am thirsty.' She opened a container of milk, gave him a drink, and covered him again." Initially this interaction seems to go according to custom, then there is a shift in verse 20. Sisera told Jael to stand watch at the entrance of her tent. If any man inquired if he was there, he told her to say no. In other words, Sisera enjoyed the sanctuary of Jael's gracious hospitality and then asked her to lie for him. Talk about a sour taste in your mouth! In Eastern culture it is shameful to turn against those who have extended hospitality to you. It is deplorable to ask your host to participate in an evil deed, like lying, on your behalf.[2]

Exhausted from battle, his stomach soothed by milk, Sisera slept soundly within the safety of Jael's tent. Judges 4:21 graphically describes what happens next: "While he was sleeping from exhaustion, Heber's wife, Jael, took a tent peg, grabbed a hammer, and went silently to Sisera. She hammered the peg into his temple and drove it into the ground, and he died." The iron chariots of Sisera were no match for the iron nail that pierced him.[3]

More than Sisera asking Jael to lie, her infamous "tent-peg-to-temple" act seemed to be fueled by a divine directive similar to that which motivated Ehud's sneak attack on King Eglon in Judges 3:16–25. I understand that plunging a sword into a blubbery king and killing an army commander with a tent peg are most unusual and disturbing. Yet we cannot overlook that these acts, clearly directed by God at that time in Israel's history, served specific purposes that He ordained in His divine wisdom. And let's not forget that these actions were a direct result of God's people shrinking back from fully possessing the land He had given them and allowing their hearts to be drawn away by the pagan cultures around them.

> The lies of men deceive us. The truth of God delivers us.

The Israelites would have been spared much heartache and turmoil if they had obeyed God's commands to destroy the Canaanites in the first place. We can do things God's way, right away, or we can experience the pain of pride, insisting we know better. If you, like me, have chosen the latter more times than you care to admit, may this quote from Matthew Henry bolster you: "better be wise late, and buy wisdom by experience, than never wise."[4]

The lies of men deceive us. The truth of God delivers us.

## Engage

Below, the right-hand column is a list of Bible verses, and the left-hand column contains a list of lies. Read the first Scripture reference on the list, then see which lie it crushes. Draw an arrow from the Scripture that directly combats that particular lie. Keep going all the way down the list. If you'd like, fight like Jael by making your arrow look like a tent peg as you confront the enemy with the permeating truth of God's Word.

| Human Lie | God's Truth |
| --- | --- |
| I cannot overcome this bad habit. | Psalm 103:8–10 |
| The Bible is flawed. | Hebrews 4:15 |
| No one understands what I'm going through. | 1 Corinthians 6:19–20 |
| I cannot be forgiven. | Psalm 19:9 |
| God is cruel and oppressive. | 1 Corinthians 10:13 |
| I can live however I want. | Psalm 103:11–12 |

This is a powerful exercise you can continue in the coming days. When you encounter a lie, ask God to show you a verse or two to combat it. If we want to walk in victory, it is essential we don't bow to the lies that threaten to enter our home and head. We need levelheaded clarity.

Judges 4:22 marks the arrival of Barak to Jael's tent. He had been pursuing Sisera. Jael greeted him and said, "Come and I will show you the man you are looking for." Barak followed her into the tent and saw Sisera lying dead, with the tent peg through his temple! Deborah's prophecy to Barak proved true in this regard as well. Not only did God lure Sisera, his chariots, and his infantry to the Wadi Kishon and hand him over to Barak

(v. 7) but Barak did not receive the honor of the kill because the Lord sold out Sisera to a woman, Jael (v. 9).

While Jael hammering a tent peg into Sisera's temple is shocking, don't miss its greater purpose. This event in Judges 4:22 is a powerful reminder of the prophecy from Gen. 3:15 that had not yet been fulfilled, when the offspring of the woman would strike our enemy's head and free us forever.

Judges 4:23 concludes our designated Bible passage for today, and it also marks the conclusion of the intense battle near Mount Tabor: "That day God subdued King Jabin of Canaan before the Israelites." God used the likes of Othniel, Ehud, Shamgar, Deborah, Barak, and Jael to clean house so that the Israelites "would not be like their ancestors, a stubborn and rebellious generation, a generation whose heart was not loyal and whose spirit was not faithful to God" (Ps. 78:8).

*God, reveal to me where I have swallowed lies . . . about You, myself, and others. I want to have levelheaded clarity and divine wisdom to discern between joint and marrow, so I can stand confidently upon Your impenetrable truth. Help me to lean in to Your compassionate love, for others and for myself. Help me love You freely and trust You fully, even when I don't understand it all. You call out sin in order to set me free. Forgive me for flirting with the enticing vices of this world. Give me an appetite for Your will and Your proven wisdom. Show me the error of my ways, so I can run in the way of Your commands (Ps. 119:32). Thank You for giving me second and third and twentieth chances to start again. Only You can change me from the inside out. I want to experience life to the fullest in a way that blesses and honors You, my Redeemer. Thank You for Your constant companionship, Your enduring patience, and Your unwavering commitment to a personal relationship with me. Help me choose You each day. When lies rise, equip me to drive Your tent peg of truth right through them. In Jesus's name, Amen.*

### Reflect

1. What is a lie you have swallowed lately?

2. Ask God to lead you to a specific Scripture that combats that lie. Record it below and work on memorizing it this week.

### Bonus

When our kids were younger, we would ask them to identify the lies that advertisers often used in commercials. For example, "If you buy this new device, you'll be accepted and respected." Give it a try this week; whether it's a song or a movie, try to spot a lie and replace it with the truth.

---

### DECIDE
When you are bombarded with lies, decide to let the truth of God's Word rise above the deception of the world.

# "God, What Do I Do When Enemies Rise Against Me?"

### ▨ *Victory in the Valley*

Deal with them as you did with Midian, as you did with Sisera and Jabin at the Kishon River.

PSALM 83:9

## Read

PSALM 83:1–18

When you find yourself in a battle of wills, gossip swirls around you, or false accusations are hurled in your direction, it can be tempting to aim angry words and even hate at those who hurt you. I am often reminded of Ephesians 6:12, "For our struggle is not against flesh and blood, but against the rulers, against the authorities, against the cosmic powers of this darkness, against evil, spiritual forces in the heavens." Even though people hurt us, there is more to it than that. The devil and his demons specialize in tripping us up, ensnaring us with unforgiveness, and confusing us about who the real enemy is. But God is greater, and Jesus has defeated sin and death. We know that the end is coming for the devil (Rev. 20:7–10). During our time on earth, what can we do about evil? How are we to respond when we face injustice? What do we ultimately want for those who oppose God? Let's look for answers in today's passage.

## Focus

We have studied Judges 4 in the last four lessons, but today we are looking at Psalm 83:1–18. It contains additional information about the battle between Barak and Sisera and how God chose to deliver victory to His people.

Psalm 83 starts with an SOS prayer from the Israelites to God. They cry out and ask Him not to be silent or deaf to the uproar of His enemies and those who hate Him and have acted in arrogance.

In Psalm 83:5, we see how the enemies of the Israelites conspired with one mind to form an alliance against God. They had the audacity to unify in thought and action against God—the covenant-keeping God who cannot and will not break covenant with His people. These enemies were intent on wiping out God's people as a nation so Israel would no longer be remembered (v. 4). They weren't the only ones who plotted the same. Even today, the conflict over Israel continues.

Many battles, laws, sins, and consequences are recorded in the Old Testament. Yet through them we clearly see humanity's desperate need for Christ. If God kept a record of sins, who could stand? With God there is forgiveness so we can serve Him (Ps. 130:3–4). Thanks be to God, who gives us the victory through Jesus Christ our Lord (1 Cor. 15:55–57).

## Engage

1. Read Psalm 103:9–18. Record the truths you find that describe God's heart and His actions toward those who are His on the following chart. (The first two verses have been filled in for you.)

### God's Heart Toward His Children (Ps. 103)

| Scripture | Action Motivated by Love |
| --- | --- |
| Verse 9 | God will not always accuse or be angry forever. |
| Verse 10 | God has not dealt with us or repaid us as our sins deserve. |

| Scripture | Action Motivated by Love |
|-----------|--------------------------|
| Verse 11 | |
| Verse 12 | |
| Verse 13 | |
| Verse 14 | |
| Verse 17 | |

2. Look back over the phrases you recorded. Which one or two offer the most comfort to you today? Circle them.

3. Now read Psalm 103:9–18 one more time and record the actions required of God's chosen people in the blanks provided below. Hint: The last two words of Psalm 103:11 contain the first action. This same action is mentioned two more times throughout this passage, in verses 13 and 17.

Verse 11  *fear*  *Him*

Verse 13   _____ _____

Verse 17   _____ _____

Verse 18   _____ _____

      _____ _____

Verse 18   _____

      _____

### God Brings the Victory

Reread Psalm 83:1–8. What was happening to God's people at the time this psalm was written? Jot down phrases below for verses 2–5. A few of them have been done as an example.

### The Times of Psalm 83:1–5

| Reference | Action |
| --- | --- |
| Verse 2 | Your enemies make an uproar. |
| Verse 2 | Those who hate God act arrogantly. |
| Verse 3 | |
| | |
| | |

| Reference | Action |
|---|---|
| Verse 3 | |
| Verse 4 | |
| Verse 5 | They conspire with one mind. |
| Verse 5 | |

### *Those Who Conspired*

Choose one of the people groups listed in Psalm 83:6–7 who conspired against God's chosen ones. After reading the provided verse(s) about that people group, jot down a few notes about what you learned. The first one is done for you.

**Psalm 83:6**

> The Ishmaelites (Genesis 25:12–18)
>
> The tents of Edom (Amos 1:11)
>
> Moab (Isaiah 16)
>
> The Hagrites (1 Chronicles 5:10)

I chose the Ishmaelites (people group). This is what I learned about them from Scripture:

- Ishmael was the son of Hagar (Sarah's slave) and Abraham.
- Ishmael's firstborn was named Nebaioth.
- Ishmael had twelve sons.

- Ishmael died when he was 137 years old.
- Ishmael's descendants settled in the area from Havilah to Shur, east of Egypt.

**Psalm 83:7**

Gebal (Ezekiel 27:9)

Ammon (Amos 1:13–15)

Amalek (Deuteronomy 25:17–18)

Philistia (1 Samuel 17)

The inhabitants of Tyre (Ezekiel 26:1–28:19)

I chose _____. This is what I learned about them in this passage:

Continue this exercise below. The rest of these verses mention one people group at a time.

**Psalm 83:8**

Assyria (2 Kings 17:1–6)

This is what I learned about the Assyrians:

**Psalm 83:9**

Midian, Sisera, and Jabin (Judges 4; you already know about them
from this week of our study! See how much you remember.)

This is what I remember about Sisera and Jabin:

**Psalm 83:10**

Those destroyed at En-dor (Joshua 17:11)

This is what I learned about those destroyed at En-dor:

**Psalm 83:11–12**

Oreb, Zeeb, Zebah, and Zalmunna (Judges 7–8)

This is what I learned about the enemies who were defeated by the Lord:

### The Rest of the Story

Understanding more about the enemies of the Israelites helps us better understand the intensity of the opposition that surrounded them during this time in history. Verses 13–15 lay out the specifics of how the Israelites would like their enemies to be dealt with:

(Verse 13) Make them like tumbleweed, like straw before the wind.

(Verse 14) Pursue them as fire burns a forest and flame blazes through mountains.

(Verse 15) Pursue them with your tempest, terrify them with your storm.

In verse 16, the Israelites ask God to cover the enemies' faces with shame, so they will seek the Lord's name. Verse 17 lays it all out: "Let them be put to shame and terrified forever; let them perish in disgrace." This is their plea for relief from their enemies. It is their cry to God, from their despair. SOS!

Have you been there? Have you felt cornered by the pressures of life? Have you wondered if things would ever get better? Have you cried out for justice and asked God to deal with those who rise up against you?

You are not alone. The Israelites were well acquainted with situations like these. They knew God could do something about it. How often do we take matters into our own hands? I have been guilty of thinking I could handle a situation better than the Most High. How foolish of me! My understanding is limited, and I see things solely through the lens of my personal experience. But there is often more to the story than we know.

Will we choose to trust God even when we don't understand? Will we believe Him even when we don't know what will happen next?

God knows the hearts of all. He sees all the angles. Think about the times He has been so outlandishly gracious to you. Sometimes we want God to be our genie in a bottle, striking down our foes with lightning and giving us our heart's desire on a silver platter. Yet He moves and acts according to infinite wisdom. He knows all, and He reigns over all. He is the Righteous Judge. God is worthy to be feared, and He is willing to be our friend. What a mystery!

Even those who oppose, mock, or persecute God's people can be recipients of this mercy. Take Saul-turned-Paul, for example (Gal. 1:11–17).

> Even those who oppose, mock, or persecute God's people can be recipients of this mercy.

At the end of Psalm 83, we read: "May they know that you alone—whose name is the Lord—are the Most High over the whole earth" (v. 18). Talk about a perspective shifter. God's people ask for justice, for recompense, but even greater is their request for God to be glorified, so their enemies will know He is the Most High. Even our enemies can experience God's salvation if they receive Him by faith. That can be a difficult concept to buy into, but let's not forget we, too, were once enemies of Christ.

God did not treat us as our sins deserved. He dealt with our sin by sacrificing His only Son, Jesus, to pay the debt we owed. He did not leave us in our depraved state; He made a way for us to be reconciled to Him, forever. Our chief aim is this: to glorify God and enjoy Him for all eternity.[1] How bountifully He has dealt with us.

## Reflect

1. Read Romans 5:10, then answer the following questions.

How was friendship with God restored?

When did Jesus die for us?

2. Read Colossians 1:21–23, then answer the following questions.

Where were the people hostile (what body part)?

How was that hostility expressed?

How can we be reconciled?

What are we to keep doing, according to verse 23?

3. Read Psalm 145:17–21 out loud:

> The LORD is righteous in all his ways
> and faithful in all he does.
> The LORD is near to all who call on him,
> to all who call on him in truth.
> He fulfills the desires of those who fear him;
> he hears their cry and saves them.
> The LORD watches over all who love him,
> but all the wicked he will destroy.
>
> My mouth will speak in praise of the LORD.
> Let every creature praise his holy name
> for ever and ever. (NIV)

## Bonus

Read Galatians 1:11–17 and think about who in your life needs a Saul-to-Paul transformation. Pray for God to do a mighty work in someone you may even consider to be an enemy—of you or of God. You have been shown mercy. Would you ask God to show them mercy as well? It might seem impossible right now, but the impossible is God's specialty.

> ## DECIDE
> When your enemies rise against you,
> decide to let God deal with them.

*Dear Jesus,*

*When I am afraid, I will put my trust in You (Ps. 56:3). When I am intimidated by the "iron chariots" of life, may I lean into Your strength and recount Your promises. Thank You that I am never truly alone, for You are very near. Give me courage to link arms with those You have led me to instead of competing with them. Show me how to collaborate in a way that honors You. Help me fix my eyes on You and not be swept away by the cares of this life.*

*You are my great Redeemer and Deliverer. You expose the lies, You right the wrongs, and Your justice rolls down like a river. Your presence is my comfort and my courage. Increase my faith in You, and may my actions put feet to my belief. Thank You for showing me mercy. You transform enemies into friends through the cleansing power of Your blood. Amen.*

# WEEK 4 WRAP-UP

*This week, I decide to rise in faith to fulfill*
*my unique purpose at this time in history.*

Answer the following questions to help summarize what you learned during this week of study. If possible, use biblical references to back up your responses.

1. Psalm 19:4–6 says, "Their message has gone out to the whole earth, and their words to the ends of the world. In the heavens he has pitched a tent for the sun. It is like a bridegroom coming from his home; it rejoices like an athlete running a course. It rises from one end of the heavens and circles to their other end; nothing is hidden from its heat." What can you glean about faithfully rising to fulfill your God-given purpose from the example of the sun as outlined in these verses?

2. What did you learn about going forward in faith, based on the Scriptures you read this week?

3. How did Barak, Deborah, and Jael each rise to the God-sized task God gave them, as recorded in Judges?

4. What are some of the benefits of collaborating with others for the kingdom?

5. Based on what you discovered in Lessons 1–5, how can the decision to rise help you make wise decisions in uncertain times?

# THE DECISION TO TESTIFY

## JUDGES 5

Now that we have studied the battle of Judges 4, it's time to celebrate with praise and thanksgiving and testify to what God has done on behalf of His people. This week we will study the song of Deborah, in Judges 5, and rejoice in the victory God delivered for His people and delivers to us daily through Jesus. You will discover that the decision to testify will strengthen your faith and the faith of those around you. It might even inspire someone to believe in Jesus for the first time. When you don't know what to do next, testifying about God will bolster your confidence in His character and His ability to come through for you and others, again and again.

**KEY VERSE: PSALM 78:4**

We will not hide them from their children,
but will tell a future generation
the praiseworthy acts of the LORD,
his might, and the wondrous works
he has performed.

# LESSON 1

# "God, What Do I Do When I've Been Delivered?"

LORD, when you came from Seir, when you marched from the fields of Edom, the earth trembled, the skies poured rain, and the clouds poured water.

JUDGES 5:4

## Read

JUDGES 5:1–7

When something significant happens in your life, it is important to acknowledge that milestone in some way, so you don't forget the amazing thing God did. Judges 5 is a memorial song, reminding the Israelites of God's deliverance on their behalf and how He helped them overcome their enemies. We learn from verse 1 that Deborah and Barak sang this song. It is thought to be one of the oldest recorded Scripture passages in the Bible.

## Focus

Our faith is fortified as we read this ancient testimony song in Judges 5. Deborah and Barak recount what God did for His people and what the people did for Him in the battle near Mount Tabor. God clearly told the Israelites to tell the next generation what He had done, so they would not turn away from Him. This song not only gives God praise for His marvelous deeds but was written to make sure current and future generations remembered His faithfulness in defeating Sisera, and ultimately Jabin.

These memorable lyrics provide "a glimpse into Israel's most important communication device: word of mouth. Much of the history and lore of Israel was committed to poetry and song for dissemination to the whole culture."[1] Think about it; we can recall lyrics to a song more easily than words not set to music. The other day a church song from childhood emerged in my mind that I haven't thought of in a while, yet it remained engrained in my memory. It is based on Exodus 15:1–3, another testimony song. After God delivered the Hebrews out of their bondage to Pharaoh, parted the Red Sea, and took care of those pursuing them, Moses sang a song of praise and thanks to remind the people about the mighty things God had done for them.

> Then Moses and the people of Israel sang this song to the LORD:
>
>> "I will sing to the LORD,
>>     for he has triumphed gloriously;
>> he has hurled both horse and rider
>>     into the sea.
>> The Lord is my strength and my song;
>>     he has given me victory.
>> This is my God, and I will praise him—
>>     my father's God, and I will exalt him!
>> The LORD is a warrior;
>>     Yahweh is his name!" (Exod. 15:1–3 NLT)

The practice of passing down these memorial songs from generation to generation was an effective way for the Israelites to solidify their remembrance of God's faithfulness and deliverance.

## Engage

1. Reread today's passage, Judges 5:1–7, then underline any reference to time (the first two are done for you):

<u>On that day</u> Deborah and Barak son of Abinoam sang:

> <u>When</u> the leaders lead in Israel,
> when the people volunteer,
> blessed be the LORD.
> Listen, kings! Pay attention, princes!
> I will sing to the LORD;
> I will sing praise to the LORD God of Israel.
> LORD, when you came from Seir,
> when you marched from the fields of Edom,
> the earth trembled,
> the skies poured rain,
> and the clouds poured water.
> The mountains melted before the LORD,
> even Sinai, before the LORD, the God of Israel.
>
> In the days of Shamgar son of Anath,
> in the days of Jael,
> the main roads were deserted
> because travelers kept to the side roads.
> Villages were deserted,
> they were deserted in Israel,
> until I, Deborah, arose,
> a mother in Israel.

2. What sticks out to you about the time references in this passage?

Judges 5:2 contains three key phrases. Let's take a closer look at each one.

**When the leaders lead in Israel . . .**

Deborah and Barak were appointed by God to lead and to fulfill unique roles at a specific time in history. "When the leaders lead in Israel" is like saying, "it is a good thing when those God calls are faithful to follow His instructions completely." We have countless examples of leaders who have fallen short, who started strong and then got derailed by apathy, pride, or compromise. Yet here we see leaders who worked together to carry out a victorious outcome for God's people, under the directive and authority of God's leadership. However, it wasn't only the leaders who made this possible.

**When the people volunteer . . .**

Deborah and Barak could not have accomplished this God-sized task—defeating the enemy—without willing volunteers. Ten thousand troops, plus many others (see verses 14, 15, and 18) came to fight alongside Barak and Deborah in this battle.

Many church leaders today are stretched too thin, trying to fill the gaps in ministry because there are not enough people willing to volunteer. When each member of the body of Christ does their part, no one part is overwhelmed by demands or atrophied through underuse.

**Blessed be the Lord.**

In this victory song, we see how the leaders and volunteers worked in harmony to accomplish God's mighty purposes. It is a marvel to onlookers when a group of people are on the same page, united in purpose to accomplish something they could never have done on their own. Blessed be the Lord!

### Songs of Praise

Judges 5:3 uses the word *shema* again (like we talked about in Week 1). Here, it is translated "Listen, kings!" or "Hear this, you kings!" In other words, "Pay attention, princes, because I am going to sing praise to the Lord God of Israel." It is interesting to note there were no kings in Israel at this time. Deborah was likely referring to the kings and princes in the surrounding nations. Her phrasing served as both a warning and an invitation to give credit to the King of kings and bow to Him alone.

Judges 5:4–5 continues to explain why the God of Israel was worthy of praise. These lyrics reveal the details of how He delivered His people from Sisera and the iron chariots.

1. Draw a picture of what the Lord did to the earth, skies, clouds, and mountains, as described in Judges 5:4–5:

2. Judges 5:6–7 begins with "In the days of Shamgar son of Anath, in the days of Jael." What insight does this give you on when these events took place?

3. Try to recall from memory what Shamgar did to deliver God's people:

4. What did Jael do to deliver God's people?

5. These verses also describe what life was like for the Israelites under the oppression of Jabin. Finish the sentences below to solidify in your mind what things looked like:

(Verse 6) The main roads were _____.

(Verse 6) Travelers kept to the _____

_____.

(Verse 7) Villages were _____ in Israel.

### Declaring What God Has Done

During this desperate time, the Philistines and the Canaanites controlled the main trade routes, so the Israelites avoided those roadways. The threat of attack marked their daily lives with fear and uncertainty.

> The instability of life in Israel at the end of the Late Bronze Age is poignantly illustrated in this passage. The roads could not be protected and made secure because there was no longer any central government to do the job. For most of the Late Bronze II era (c. 1400–1200 BC) the Egyptians had given up on their pretensions to empire. Israel was certainly not a central power in any sense of the word and had little overall influence on the situation. Village life consisted of the families who lived on the land, namely, subsistence farmers and stockkeepers who provided food for marketplaces in larger cities. A secure village life was essential for the stability of the overall economy.[2]

The end of verse 7 basically says, "This is how things were—bleak and dismal, a time of fear, despair, and oppression—until I, Deborah, arose, a mother in Israel."

Deborah took her place in protecting, exhorting, and caring for those God entrusted to her. It was daunting, it was difficult, it was daring. Deborah rose to the occasion with the mandate God gave and the strength He supplied. She acknowledged her role in the process but gave God credit for the victory.

When God delivered the Hebrews from Pharaoh by parting the Red Sea, allowing them to pass through while throwing the enemy's horses and riders into the sea, Miriam led the people in a song of praise and thanksgiving (Exod. 15:19–21). When God delivered the Israelites from Jabin by sweeping his troops away in the Kishon, Deborah led the people in a song of praise and thanksgiving (Judg. 5:1).

> Deborah rose to the occasion with the mandate God gave and the strength He supplied.

Isn't it fascinating that Miriam sang a song of praise after God's deliverance and Deborah did too? This was part of their tradition. It was an effective way to pass down their history and remind one another and future generations about the faithfulness of God. (Don't worry, I am not going to ask you to pen lyrics to memorialize what you have learned from this study, but of course you are more than welcome to do so if you'd like.)

Deborah's song proclaims God's power to His people in the past and present:

> Lord, when you came from Seir,
> when you marched from the fields of Edom,
> the earth trembled,
> the skies poured rain,
> and the clouds poured water.
> The mountains melted before the Lord,
> even Sinai, before the Lord, the God of Israel. (Judg. 5:4–5)

In Charles Spurgeon's sermon on Judges 5:11, he explains that Deborah sang about the overthrow of Israel's enemies, but

> we have a far richer theme for music; we have been delivered from worse enemies, and saved by a greater salvation. Let our gratitude be deeper; let our song be more jubilant. Glory be unto God, we can say that our sins, which were like mighty hosts, have been swept away, not by that ancient river, the river Kishon, but by streams which flowed from Jesus's side. Our great enemy has been overcome, and his head is broken. Not Sisera, but Satan has been overthrown: the "seed of the woman has bruised his head" forever. We are now ransomed from the galling yoke; we walk at liberty through the power of the great Liberator, the Lord Jesus.[3]

I can't help but think of Mary's song in the New Testament, as recorded in Luke 1:46–55. The time had come for God to send the Deliverer, Jesus, to recuse all His people once and for all, to drown their sin in His blood, to provide a permanent way out of the enemy's oppression. Mary, with Jesus in her womb, offered a song to testify of His ultimate deliverance.

Miriam sang about the deliverance from slavery under Pharaoh, Deborah sang about the deliverance from oppression under Sisera, and Mary sang about the mercy of God toward His people, the fulfillment of His covenantal promise through Jesus (vv. 54–55). That fact that Jesus has delivered us from the enemy of our souls and washed away our sins completely should cause us to offer shouts of praise and overflow with thanksgiving.

Our response should be a surrendered life, where we say a resounding yes and follow Him even to the ends of the earth, knowing He is with us and for us. Jesus is worth it and worthy of it all!

The songs of Miriam, Deborah, and Mary reminded each of these women what God had done for them, but it didn't end there. These testimony songs were meant to remind others around them what God had done—and to remind us.

> **Now it's your turn to declare what God has done for you. If you haven't already, head over to KatieMReid .com/Judges to access the Bible study playlist and pour out praise to the Liberator of your life!**

## Reflect

Time on earth is measured by seconds, minutes, hours, days, weeks, months, seasons, and years. As each year comes to an end, it is a good practice to reflect on what God has done in, through, and around you. You might not pen a song to recount His faithfulness, but it strengthens your faith to pause and thank God for what He has done over these last few weeks in your life as you have studied Judges.

1. Finish the sentence below:
   *Thank you, God, for*

2. Record a time when you have witnessed people coming together under the banner of God's instructions and His authority to carry out a God-sized task. What was done, and how did it impact others?

## Bonus

Read Exodus 15 in its entirety. Read Luke 1:46–55 and record a few key points below:

---

### DECIDE

When you have been delivered, decide to testify about God's deliverance and His goodness.

# "God, What Do I Do to Encourage Those Around Me?"

Let them tell the righteous acts of the LORD, the righteous deeds of his villagers in Israel, with the voices of the singers at the watering places. Then the LORD's people went down to the city gates.

JUDGES 5:11

## Read

JUDGES 5:8–11

What's the best way to encourage those around you—especially those who find themselves in a challenging season? I have several friends who have the spiritual gift of encouragement. They literally put courage in me when I'm floundering or need a lift. God has gifted them with an ability to help others keep going with their timely, bolstering words. Today's passage leads with correction and is followed by encouragement. Both can motivate us toward change when offered from a place of love.

## Focus

Deborah and Barak's song of testimony continues. In Judges 5:8, they give the reason for the war the Israelites experienced: "Israel chose new gods." Although this song is full of faith-building declarations, let's not miss the warning that is given.

When we choose to worship "little g" gods, allowing our heart and mind to be drawn away and fixed on lesser things than almighty God, we open the door to compromise and captivity.

Maybe your idol is not a literal statue like the golden calf (Exod. 32) and it doesn't require animal sacrifice or sexual promiscuity, like Baal and Ashtoreth worship did. However, you might be bowing down to the idol of comfort, giving the best of your day to mindless scrolling or questionable entertainment. Perhaps you are incorporating New Age beliefs into your faith, idolizing a political candidate, or treating your significant other or a dear friend as your god. Don't be drawn away by lesser things, by the things that entice but lead you straight into captivity. God has freed you; don't run back to slavery.

## Engage

1. Look up the following passages and record the destructive pattern you see among God's people regarding following other gods:

Judges 2:12–13

Judges 2:17

Judges 10:6

Deuteronomy 32:16–17

### *The Five* C's

Let's look further into Judges 5:8. Because the people chose new gods, there was war in their city gates. They had no shield or spear to hand. They had turned from God's ways, followed their fleshly impulses, and were drawn away by the idol worship of those around them. Without God's merciful, divine intervention, they were defenseless against the enemy.

Have you ever tried to minimize or conceal your sin, only to discover that anguish grew within you? When we choose to do what is wrong, heaviness grows. It doesn't feel good, so we deflect, we rationalize, we deceive ourselves, turning a blind eye to that which is seen and known by God.

Our heavenly Father is looking down with love upon His children. He is not an absentee dad or a disinterested one. He is present and attentive. His love is protective and lavish and just. He desires your heart to be His alone. He is ready to welcome you back with open arms when you fail. Jesus was crucified on the cross so that any of our sins, even the most grievous, can be fully forgiven.

Read Psalm 32:3–7 and notice the progression in these verses:

> (Verse 3) When I was silent about my sin—when I **compromised** by disregarding your commands and pretended it was fine, I groaned and suffered.
> (Verse 4) Your **conviction** was heavy upon me, and my strength waned.
> (Verse 5) I acknowledged my sin to You. I did not cover it up but **confessed** to You, Lord, and You forgave the guilt of my sin.
> (Verse 6) I will **commit** to faithfully praying to You and seeking You. You will keep me from the reach of mighty waters that want to sweep me away.
> (Verse 7) My hiding place is in You, Lord. You **comfort** me and protect me. You sing over me and surround me with songs of deliverance.

When we compromise and wander from God's ways, we can be restored to Him through the conviction of sin, confessing our sin to God, committing to prayer, seeking His presence, and tucking under His protective wing for comfort and deliverance.

### Entrusted with Much

In Judges 5:9, we again see the repeated concept of being "with" or "for" one another: "My heart is *with* the leaders of Israel, with the volunteers of the people. Blessed be the Lord!" (emphasis added).

Deborah acknowledged her deep gratitude to those who led the army and those who volunteered to fight in the battle against Sisera. Their immense sacrifice did not go unnoticed. She called out their courage and praised God for their willingness to act.

A little appreciation goes a long way, doesn't it? It buoys us and inspires us to keep going and do more of that which has been praised.

In verse 10, Deborah addresses those who are well off and those who have little. Her exhortation is the same for various economic groups: "give praise!" In other words, "Open your mouth and speak, sing, testify about the goodness of God, who has acted mightily on your behalf and delivered you from the clutches of the enemy!"

Whether we feel we have a lot or a little, we are called to give God praise for His greatness, provision, and protection.

If you don't have a lot, you have an opportunity to *feel* your dependence on God in ways that others don't. You may be more aware of the specific ways He provides because you're relying on Him to supply your material needs. If you have been entrusted with much, it is a weighty responsibility. Take care that your material wealth does not numb you to your desperate need for God. Listen carefully to God's instructions for stewarding the abundance, caring for others, and giving Him thanks as you recognize what you have is a gift from Him to be enjoyed, shared, and multiplied for the sake of the kingdom.

> Whether we feel we have a lot or a little, we are called to give God praise for His greatness, provision, and protection.

God cares for all His children and deeply loves each one. He calls us to different things and entrusts us with varying talents and responsibilities, yet we have this in common: we are created to praise Him. Regardless of your economic or social status, sing to Him, serve Him, testify about who He is and what He has done. Then stand back and watch your faith grow!

### At the Watering Places

Judges 5:11 begins, "Let them tell the righteous acts of the Lord," and continues by describing "the righteous deeds of his villagers in Israel," which are proclaimed with "the voices of the singers at the watering places."

"Watering places" were common gathering places for the community where they filled up on the water they needed and also caught up on the latest news. Precept Austin's commentary on Judges 5 explains further, "The gates in ancient Israel were the site of legal and business activity, and so would also be the logical place to muster of troops."[1] In modern times this might be like a city hall or town square. Verse 11 ends with this: "Then the Lord's people went down to the city gates." We don't have to wait for testimony time at church to proclaim what God has done in, through, and around us. We can declare His goodness at the office water cooler, over coffee with a friend, during a neighborhood walk, and around the dinner table. Whether we're at the watering places or the city gates, we can tell of God's mighty acts and the righteous deeds of others as we go about everyday life. When others see how God is with us and has brought us through difficult times, they take notice, even if they don't yet believe in Him. When they hear about the generosity of others who have taken care of a need in our lives, they are encouraged. But how will they know unless we tell them?

Sharing about what God has done for us can feel scary or intimidating, but it can be simple, and it gets easier the more we do it.

### Say So

Here are some ideas about how and when to testify to God's work in your life:

- "Say so." (See where God is at work around you and say so. A good time to do this is while driving in the car with family or friends. For example, "Wow! Look at the sunset God made this morning.")
- Bring it up in conversation.
- Mention it in the grocery store line.
- Write it in a card or letter.
- Send a text or write a post.
- Display it on clothing, with a bumper sticker, or in your decor.
- Speak up during testimony time at church.
- Mention it over a meal.

My friend Kate Motaung wrote a book called *Share Your Story: The Transforming Power of Telling Others What God Has Done*. When I interviewed Kate on *The Martha + Mary Show*, she offered this helpful framework for testifying to what God has done in your life.[2]

### Kate's Framework for Sharing Your Story

| 1. Trial | Share a trial or experience you faced or a sinful behavior you struggled with. |
|---|---|
| 2. Provision | Share how God helped you or provided for you in the midst of that trial or experience. |
| 3. Impact | Share how God's help and intervention impacted your daily life. |
| 4. Hope | Share a message of hope or encouragement for someone going through a similar experience. |

### Put Courage in Others

As we saw in Judges 5:11, we are to testify of God's goodness and tell what He has done through others. We encourage—put courage into others—when we call out their faithfulness. We build them up when we take notice and express to them how their actions are spurring us on.

As a parent, I find it can be easier to focus on what my children are doing wrong than what they are doing right. However, when I discipline myself to call out the good I see in them, I give them a much better motivator for redirection than always being on their case. Isn't that true in our lives too? When someone expresses appreciation for the good deeds we have done, the gracious way we responded, or the sacrifice we made, it encourages us to do more of the same. When we feel seen, valued, and thanked, it motivates us to rise to the occasion.

> When you see a willing volunteer bravely carrying out what God has asked of them, say so! It might be what they need to keep going.

When you see a willing volunteer bravely carrying out what God has asked of them, say so! It might be what they need to keep going.

Is there someone in your life you can encourage today by testifying to the way God has worked through them? Your encouragement can further mobilize them in carrying out their God-given purpose: to praise Him, to walk with Him, to follow His directives with joy.

Don't delay; express your gratitude to them today!

**Reflect**

1. What people, things, or practices have captured your affections more than God?

2. Take a moment right now to ask God if there is an area in your life where you have compromised and are trying to conceal it. While it is uncomfortable to be called out in our sin, it is the first step to repentance, which leads to restoration. Walk through the steps illustrated below, regarding this specific area in your life, and rejoice in His willingness to forgive you, separate you from your sin "as far as the east is from the west" (Ps. 103:12), and surround you with songs of deliverance!

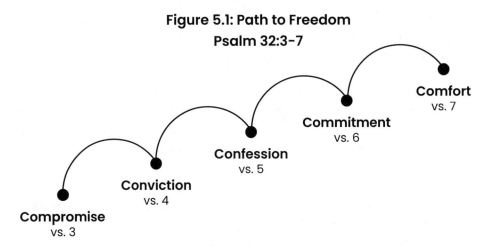

**Figure 5.1: Path to Freedom**
**Psalm 32:3-7**

Comfort
vs. 7

Commitment
vs. 6

Confession
vs. 5

Conviction
vs. 4

Compromise
vs. 3

**Bonus**

Read Psalm 103:8–13. Which truth from this passage are you the most thankful for today?

> ## DECIDE
> When you want to encourage those around you,
> decide to testify about what God has done through them.

# "God, What Do I Do When Someone Has Let Me Down?"

The princes of Issachar were with Deborah; Issachar was with Barak; they were under his leadership in the valley. There was great searching of heart among the clans of Reuben.

JUDGES 5:15

## Read

JUDGES 5:12–18

Has someone let you down recently? If so, I'm sorry. No one likes the feeling of dashed hopes or unmet expectations—when we're counting on someone to come through and they ghost us or flat out refuse to help with a pressing need. We might be tempted to shake someone and say, "Wake up! Rise up! We need you. We can't do this without you." Could it be that's how Barak and Deborah felt toward some of the tribes of Israel in the heat of battle against Sisera's army?

## Focus

Awake! Arise! Rouse from sleep, be watchful, be alert, be positioned to act!

In Judges 5:12, the word *awake* is mentioned four times in reference to Deborah. A similar word, *arise*, is used in reference to Barak, instructing him to take his prisoners. These exhortations are reminders of the swift action of these two leaders against the enemy.

*Awake.*

*Arise.*

I fear the ease and comfort of Western culture, with its constant access to endless distractions and mind-numbing behaviors, has lulled us to sleep in a spiritual sense. Our brains are being reprogrammed as we get our next quick fix, trying to avoid pain and escape the void we feel. Our attention spans are decreasing, our anxiety is increasing. This isn't a time to mince words or sugarcoat reality. It is time to come out of our stupor and awaken our natural and spiritual senses to what God is doing! Time is short, there is a battle at hand, and you need to rise to your God-given position as His child and faithfully carry out your divine directives. There are hurting people all around you who need the hope you have encountered: the risen Christ!

## Engage

Read the following Scriptures and write down what you learn about the concept of being awake spiritually and living in a way that honors Christ.

Malachi 4:1–3

Romans 13:11–14

Ephesians 5:1–15

We rise from death to life through Christ. We remain spiritually alert through an abiding, ongoing relationship with Him.

We have established the importance of proclaiming what God has done in order to give Him the praise due His name, strengthen our faith, and encourage those around us. As we use our words in this way, it is important we do so with honesty and humility. Our words have power, so let's use them to uplift, build up, speak truth, and encourage.

Appreciation and affirmation are not the same as flattery. Flattery is "excessive and insincere praise, given especially to further one's own interests."[1] Flattery is self-serving and can negatively affect the one giving it and the one receiving it.

> We rise from death to life through Christ. We remain spiritually alert through an abiding, ongoing relationship with Him.

In the valley times of life, we often feel the most vulnerable and exposed. We may be tempted to retreat or turn to something or someone else who can help us escape the pending battle. But it's best to follow the Lord instead of being led astray by empty promises of the enemy, who tries to woo us away with counterfeit light and a lying tongue, setting a trap to destroy us.

When we testify, we are to speak the truth, so help us God! Judges 5:13–15, 18 points out the groups of people who engaged in the battle alongside Barak and Deborah. Think of it as a thank-you list, like when an actor gives a speech at an award show, gratefully acknowledging those who've helped along the way.

1. Make a list of who came to Barak's and Deborah's aid in battle:

   (Verse 14) Those with their roots in Amalek came from

   E_____

   (Verse 14) B_____ came with

   your people after you.

   (Verse 14) The leaders came down from M_____

   (Verse 14) Those who carry a marshal's staff came from

   Z_____

   (Verse 15) The princes of I_____

   were with Deborah.

   (Verse 18) The people of Z_____

   defied death.

   (Verse 18) N_____ also, on the

   heights of the battlefield.

2. In verses 15–17, we read about the clans who did not show up and did not come to the aid of those in battle. Record who they were below:

   (Verse 16) There was great searching of heart among the clans of

   R_____.

(Verse 17) G_____ remained beyond the Jordan.

(Verse 17) D_____, why did you linger at the ships?

(Verse 17) A_____ remained at the seashore.

## Under Authority

Judges 5:15 talks about the princes of Issachar and how they were with Deborah and under Barak's leadership in the valley. In other words, they willingly put themselves under his authority, following his lead and trusting his instructions. Many in our culture bristle at the idea of being under anyone's authority. It could be because they want to call the shots and be their own boss and not have anyone tell them what to do or how to do it, or they may be suspicious of the motives of those in leadership positions or have experienced an abuse of power. While these are real issues to address and work through, I want to gently offer that willingly putting yourself under God's authority is a wise move. There is protection and blessing that come from tucking under His wing. It takes great strength to do so.

## A Great Searching of Heart

Judges 5:15–16 says, "There was great searching of heart among the clans of Reuben. Why did you sit among the sheep pens listening to the playing of pipes for the flocks? There was great searching of heart among the clans of Reuben."

The yard of my childhood home was full of oak trees, which shed their brown leaves each fall. Often it would rain, leaving the mounds of leaves heavy and wet. It was a daunting task to rake the yard, and my parents would elicit our help. I wish I could say I cheerfully obliged, but like the clans of Reuben, I avoided the unpleasant task, not by listening to music like they did but with *long* water and bathroom breaks. I remember watching my parents and siblings working outside through the kitchen window while I took my time with yet another break. I let them work hard while I "searched my heart" (a.k.a. made excuses for not doing much when they needed me).

### Renew Your Resolve

In the midst of her victory song of praise to God in Judges 5, Deborah called out those who did not engage in the battle. She testified against them. She held them accountable by pointing out their desertion. It had to be uncomfortable to hear others singing of their mistake, yet it served as a warning not to repeat that mistake again. In some ways it was an invitation to do better next time. When we blow it, it is tempting to despair and wallow in our failings, yet we can awake and arise at any time, even after a long history of mistakes. Today, we can renew our resolve to show up and follow through on and for who and what God has entrusted us with.

> When we blow it, it is tempting to despair and wallow in our failings, yet we can awake and arise at any time, even after a long history of mistakes.

Flattering lips do not advance us. But an honest assessment can help us identify blind spots and weak areas so we can learn from our shortcomings, grow healthier, and make a better choice the next time.

When someone holds you accountable, you may become defensive or distant. But if you choose to view their accountability as protective and a blessing, their honesty can lead you to humility, which leads to necessary changes in behavior.

Speaking of which, if my parents had not recently moved to a condo where the yard work is taken care of, I think I'd be volunteering to rake a whole lot of oak leaves!

## Reflect

1. Similarly to the princes of Issachar, will you choose to be under God's leadership in the valley? What might that look like?

2. Is there a task, project, or conversation you are avoiding because it is daunting? If so, what is it?

3. What is keeping you from fully following Jesus's lead?

## Bonus

Read Psalm 12:1–8 and pay attention to the contrast between flattering lips and the words of the Lord. Make some notes about what you want to remember.

**DECIDE**
When someone has let you down, decide to testify
with honest scales and a humble heart.

# "God, What Do I Do When I'm Outnumbered?"

The stars fought from the heavens; the stars fought with Sisera from their paths.

JUDGES 5:20

## Read

JUDGES 5:19–23

Have you ever felt like the odds were stacked against you? That there was no earthly way you could succeed apart from divine intervention? My school board race is like that. I am trying to stay positive, but there are obstacles in the way. A few loud voices hurl insults while others signal their approval of the hurtful words through likes, comments, and shares. Even though our flesh may want to fight back with similar tactics when provoked, what would it look like to entrust ourselves to God's keeping and let Him deal with the opposition? What if we try things God's way, letting Him lead and light our next step? God might surprise us with the way He supernaturally intervenes on our behalf, like He did with those in today's passage.

## Focus

Barak and his troops were outnumbered. The earthly odds were not in their favor. The enemy's iron chariots could flatten them. On their own strength, Barak, Deborah, and the ten thousand troops would fail. They needed divine intervention to confront the darkness that threatened to take them out.

In Judges 4:14–16, we read about Barak pursuing and overthrowing Sisera's army. This was no small thing! Let's read it again to review:

> Then Deborah said to Barak, "Go! This is the day the LORD has handed Sisera over to you. Hasn't the LORD gone before you?" So Barak came down from Mount Tabor with ten thousand men following him. The LORD threw Sisera, all his charioteers, and all his army into a panic before Barak's assault. Sisera left his chariot and fled on foot. Barak pursued the chariots and the army as far as Harosheth of the Nations, and the whole army of Sisera fell by the sword; not a single man was left.

## Engage

Pay attention to the action words in the passage above to help you answer the following questions:

1. What did Deborah do in Judges 4:14?

2. What did Barak do in Judges 4:15–16?

3. What did God do in Judges 4:15?

4. Deborah, Barak, and God each played an active role in the battle. While they all had an important role, who ultimately commanded Barak to engage in this fight and secured the victory? (Hint: verse 14 contains the answer.)

5. Since Israel did not have any kings at this time, which kings fought in the battle according to Judges 5:19? And whose side were they on?

6. Where did they fight?

7. Why did they not "plunder the silver"? Plundering was a common part of war. Why do you think they did not do it?

### Stars Fought from the Heavens

Deborah declared that the stars fought from the heavens and fought Sisera from their paths (Judg. 5:20). It is likely God caused thunder, lightning, rain, and hailstones to fall from the sky, as He had done to thwart Israel's enemies at other times.

In verse 21, continuing the theme of God executing judgment through nature, we read about the ancient Wadi Kishon sweeping away Jabin's army. The water of Kishon was usually quite shallow, yet the downpour created a flash flood that wiped out the opposition. Here we see the fulfillment of God's promise in Judges 4:7: "Then I will lure Sisera commander of Jabin's army, his chariots, and his infantry at the Wadi Kishon to fight against you, and I will hand him over to you." The Creator utilized His creation to execute power over Israel's enemies.

> The Creator utilized His creation to execute power over Israel's enemies.

God used His reign of nature to deliver the Hebrews from slavery in Egypt—a pillar of cloud, a pillar of fire, the parting of the Red Sea. In Judges 4–5, God used nature again to provide triumph for His people over their enemies. Throughout Scripture, we see examples of how "God employed nature both to bless His people for their faith and obedience, and to curse them for their rebellion."[1] In other words, God, who rules over all, can use nature to draw people to Him whether through its beauty or through its destruction. Why? So they will know He is the Lord.

A breathtaking sunset inspires my heart to worship the Creator, and a terrifying lightning flash fills me with the fear of the Lord faster than just about anything.

The Creator continually utilizes nature to express His abundant love to us.

1. Read the following verses about God's work through His creation. Write down the main points below or write down one of the verses in each passage that stands out to you.

   Psalm 19:1–4

   Romans 1:18–19

   Job 38:1–18, 34–38

2. Read the following verses (if you are short on time, choose two) and take note of how God used nature to accomplish His purposes.

   Deuteronomy 11:8–17

Exodus 15:3–12

Joshua 10:9–11

1 Samuel 7:10

### March On, My Soul

My friend and I were on a road trip when she told me about the floodwaters of addiction that threatened to sweep away her marriage. She confessed she wanted to get a tattoo that said, "March on, my soul, in strength." It was a fitting phrase to describe the stamina she needed for the upcoming battle.

This ancient declaration, sung by the prophetess and judge Deborah in Judges 5:21, resonated deeply with my bold and beautiful friend. She had been blindsided by this difficult circumstance, and supernatural resolve was required to face the uncertainty before her. She wanted a permanent reminder inked upon skin and heart as she soldiered on.

Regardless of our individual stances on tattoos, I think we can agree that strength is required to navigate this present age. But I am not simply referring to physical stamina; mental sharpness and spiritual sensitivity are also needed. Ecclesiastes 7:19 says, "Wisdom makes the wise person stronger than ten rulers of a city." Don't you want this kind of inner strength when you are confronted with injustice? This stronger-than-ten-rulers robustness? My road trip friend does, and so do I. We do not just want a catchphrase to display on a phone screen or etch into our forearm; we want this type of soul strength to mark our daily choices; infuse our homes, work, and church life; and positively influence coming generations.

Proverbs 9:10–12 contains the answer to where wisdom is found and the rich blessing that accompanies it:

> The fear of the LORD is the beginning of wisdom,
> and the knowledge of the Holy One is understanding.
> For by me your days will be many,
> and years will be added to your life.
> If you are wise, you are wise for your own benefit;
> if you mock, you alone will bear the consequences.

It is wise to revere the God of the universe. Endless insight is found in Him. It is smart to apply His truth to daily life—whether we are on the mountaintop, in the valley, or somewhere in between.

Judges 5:21 is probably the most famous line in Deborah's song: "March on, my soul, in strength." As the battle rages, press on and don't give up. Rely on the One who knows all. Let God testify against the opposition as you follow His marching orders.

As you agree with what God calls light and what He deems as darkness—and don't mix up the two—you are aligning yourself with the star-breathing, DNA-weaving Creator, who infused value into your being before you could lift a finger. You are acknowledging His right to rule and reign over your life. He can be trusted. His character is flawless; His ways are just. He makes all things new. Does He sometimes use unconventional ways to get our attention or accomplish His purposes? Yes! But the Lord knows what He is doing. He knows best, and He knows you better than anyone—including yourself.

God sees the big picture and the minute details. He reigns over all—over creation, over the enemy, over what you are battling right now, over every injustice.

Ask God to rally your soul to respond in faith, "March on, my soul, in strength" (v. 21).

### A Shift in the Song

Judges 5:22 mentions that the horses' hooves of Jabin's army hammered and the stallions galloped. Can you picture it? The unrest, the chaos of the torrential rainstorm, the flashes of lightning, the soldiers shouting as the force of the river stopped their advance against Israel?

Verse 23 reveals that the angel of the Lord was present in this fight. "'Curse Meroz,' says the angel of the LORD, 'Bitterly curse her inhabitants, for they did not come to help the LORD, to help the LORD with the warriors.'"

This is a shift in the song, as the angel of the Lord interjected a curse upon Meroz. Deborah reiterated this curse in the lyrics, but she was not the author of this judgment. The one true Judge was, and He judges rightly.

Did the Lord *need* the people of Meroz to help Him with the victory? No, but they were called upon and expected to engage in the conflict, not avoid it. Commentators suggest that Meroz was likely closest to the battle site, so their desertion in this time of need was especially grievous.[2] God uses imperfect people to accomplish His perfect purposes. Our cooperation and participation in His kingdom work shapes and sanctifies us.

> God uses imperfect people to accomplish His perfect purposes. Our cooperation and participation in His kingdom work shapes and sanctifies us.

Psalm 50:4–7 builds upon the foundation of God being judge and in charge of creation. He is more mighty than we realize. Not only did He create the heavens and the earth but He summons heaven and earth to judge His people. The heavens proclaim His righteousness. We are reminded about God's holiness through His displays of power in nature.

Last night, my eleven-year-old son and I had to cross a field during a storm at camp. The lightning did not let up as we made our way from one building to the next. The strobing light flashes in the night sky punctuated the worship song we'd sung moments earlier. God is the light in the darkness. In lilting birdsong and roaring waterfall, He speaks both in whispers and shouts. His reign over nature causes us to call out to Him when we are afraid and draw near to Him when we are awed. God uses whatever He will—jarring lightning bolts and soothing sunsets—to bring all people to Himself. Judgment and beauty through nature display His glory, declaring He is God; there is no other like Him.

## Reflect

1. Maybe all this talk about God using nature to judge wrongdoing is making you uncomfortable. If so, ask yourself why you feel this way. Why does God use nature to judge those on the earth?

2. List three ways God uses nature to bless you:

3. One of my favorite psalms is Psalm 121, which speaks of God as our Creator, reminding us that our help is from Him. Read its comforting words and jot down what you learn about God:

4. Read Psalm 32:6–11, which offers comfort and loving instruction about what to do in uncertain times. What do you learn about trust from this passage?

"[Our] help comes from the LORD, the Maker of heaven and earth" (Ps. 121:2). It can be tempting to be driven by lengthy to-do lists, relying on our own ability to muscle through the day instead of keeping our eyes on the One who formed us and flung the stars into space. Our very breath comes from God. Any strength, talent, and good thing we have is a result of His divine design and mercy. When we lift our eyes to Him throughout the day, we are reminded of His character and willingness to help us with whatever we are facing.

Rest assured; God is in charge. He is always available to us, never tires, and knows the way we should go. He is the guardian and overseer of our souls (1 Pet. 2:25). He watches over us with His loving eye upon each of us.

Is there an area in your life in which you feel outnumbered, like the earthly odds are stacked against you? Do you feel vulnerable and exposed? Are you in a place where you need God to shelter you in the midst of a fiery circumstance? Psalm 121 also talks about God being our shelter (v. 5). Verse 6 says, "the sun will not strike you by day or the moon by night." God is available to shelter you from that which is intended to harm you. Psalm 91:4–5 says, "He will cover you with his feathers; you will take refuge under his wings. His faithfulness will be a protective shield. You will not fear the terror of the night, the arrow that flies by day."

The Creator of heaven and earth—*and you*—delights to provide what you need. He is the God who helps you.[3]

March on . . .

**Bonus**

Read Psalm 104 in its entirety. Don't rush. Take your time and picture the vivid imagery of God's handiwork rolled out like a scroll before you—a glorious display of creativity and love.

If you're so inclined, sketch what comes to mind as you sit with these verses.

## DECIDE

When you are outnumbered, decide to let God testify against the opposition.

## LESSON 5

# "God, What Do I Do When I Experience Peace?"

Most blessed of women is Jael, the wife of Heber the Kenite; she is most blessed among tent-dwelling women.

JUDGES 5:24

### Read

JUDGES 5:24–31

If we are used to living in a constant state of stress, worry, or discouragement, it can feel strange to experience peace. While we may have been craving peace all along, it can feel uncomfortable because we aren't used to it. We might also be concerned that the peaceful feeling or our calm circumstances are only temporary, so it may be difficult to enter into peace because we're guarded, or we are skeptical that it will last.

Peace is found in Jesus, and it flows from a personal relationship with Him and living out our identity as His beloved children. Peace isn't only what He provides; it's who He is. Peace isn't a destination; peace is Jesus. While God used temporary deliverers, in the form of judges, to help His people, He sent Jesus as our permanent Deliverer to free us from the oppression of sin and give us lasting soul rest—not just for a day or decades but forever.

## Focus

I can't wait to talk about the connection between Judges and the greater gospel story. But before we dig into our final day of study, I want to take a moment to call out the faithfulness I see in you. I am proud of you for seeing this study through! More than a checkmark on your to-do list, I hope this last day of studying Judges serves as a reflective pause, a moment of *Selah* in which all your time of study pays off.

Feel good about what you have done. Celebrate! You have set aside time to connect with God and study the Bible. Well done! I pray you have been changed, for good, through the process. I hope your appetite to feast on God's Word has increased, and your relationship with the Lord has been fortified. No matter what decisions you are faced with, you can follow Jesus daily, leaning into His time-tested wisdom for living, found within the pages of Scripture. Through the power and direction of His Holy Spirit, you can experience the unending peace He alone provides.

Judges 5 is a testimony song that declares the faithfulness of God to deliver His people from the oppression of Jabin. As the song nears its end, verses 24–27 recount Jael's faithfulness to act valiantly in the face of battle by killing Sisera. Her attack on the enemy ushered in peace. *Selah*.

Like the tour guide kept highlighting Deborah during my visit to Israel, as I mentioned in the introduction, God has been highlighting Jael throughout this study. Her extraordinary bravery contributed to the deliverance of God's people, yet I didn't understand the full weight of her actions until today. It's so exciting!

## Engage

By way of review, answer the following questions based on Judges 5:24:

1. What adjective is used to describe Jael in the opening of this verse?

2. Who is Jael's husband, and what nomadic tribe is he from?

3. In what kind of home did Jael and her husband live?

4. The details of Jael's interactions with Sisera are sung in Judges 5:25–26. What did Jael give Sisera to drink?

5. Jael used a common household object to kill Sisera; what was it?

6. Verse 26 leaves no question: Sisera is dead. Write out this verse below. It might seem gruesome, but hang in there; it will help drive a deeper point in a moment.

7. What do you have in hand to crush the deception of the enemy?

### God's Grand Plan of Deliverance

It is interesting to note that although Deborah and Barak are main characters in Judges 4–5, and they both do "big" things on God's behalf, it is Jael who receives great honor and blessing at the end of this testimony song. Sometimes we focus on the prominent followers of Christ who are doing "big" things for God. However, throughout Scripture, we often see God using those who are ordinary, humble, and even overlooked—the ones who faithfully serve Him day after day, regardless of whether others take notice. Matthew Henry's commentary describes this well:

> How honourably does [Deborah] speak of Jael who preferred her peace with the God of Israel before her peace with the king of Canaan. [Jael jeopardized] her life as truly as if she had been in the high places of the field, and bravely fought for those whom she saw God fought for. Those whose lot is cast in the tent, in a very low and narrow sphere of activity, if they serve God in that according to their capacity, shall in no way lose their reward. Jael in the tent wins as rich a blessing as Barak in the field.[1]

In Judges 5:24, Deborah sang, "Most blessed of women is Jael, the wife of Heber the Kenite; she is most blessed among tent-dwelling women." The reason for this declaration was because Jael courageously carried out the divine directive God gave her to stop Sisera, the enemy of God's people.

Our focus verse for today's lesson reminds me of a similar phrase used to describe another woman in Scripture, this time from the New Testament. In Luke 1:42, Elizabeth said this of Mary, Jesus's mother: "Blessed are you among women, and your child will be blessed!" This greeting was because Mary courageously carried the divine child given by God to stop the devil, the enemy of God's people.

Jael, like Mary, was going about her daily business without fanfare when God chose her to be a part of His grand plan for deliverance. May our response to God's specific instructions be similar to Mary's: "See, I am the Lord's servant. . . . May it happen to me as you have said" (v. 38).

Mary cooperated with her Creator, willing to be a part of His merciful provision to "proclaim release to the captives and recovery of sight to the blind, to set free the oppressed" through Christ (4:18). Jael did something similar for her people when she "crushed [Sisera's] head; she shattered and pierced his temple" (Judg. 5:26).

Read Genesis 3:1–15 to remind you of another situation where the enemy's head would be crushed. The woman mentioned in verse 15 is Mary, Jesus's mother, not Eve: "I will put hostility between you and the woman, and between your offspring and her offspring. He will strike your head, and you will strike his heel."

Jael's valiant act against Sisera was foreshadowing how Christ would fulfill this prophecy given by God about the devil's demise. This blows my mind—the gospel story is right here in Judges!

No wonder God has illuminated Jael to us. Her bold and brave act of obedience greatly helped her people, rescuing them from the clutches of the enemy, but it also served a greater purpose by pointing to the coming Savior who would render the enemy defenseless, crushing his head like God promised in the garden! Jesus did this by dying for us, allowing the nails to be driven into His hands and feet in order to purchase our freedom. Jesus allowed Himself to be "pierced for our transgressions" (Isa. 53:5 NIV) to pay for our sins and win the victory over the enemy of our souls.

He is indeed worthy to be praised!

We are not to worship or idolize Jael or Mary, but we can thank and praise God for their example, availability, willingness, devotion, and boldness in saying yes to partnering with the God of the universe for the benefit of humanity.

To recap:

- In **Genesis,** a prophetic promise is given by God that the woman's child will crush the head of the serpent.
- In **Judges,** we see a powerful foreshadowing of this coming event through Jael crushing Sisera's head.
- In the **Gospels,** God provides this promised child, Jesus, and He crushes the devil by dying for the sins of the world and rising again—defeating death and making the way for restoration between us and God.
- In **Revelation,** we see a vision of the spiritual battle in the heavenlies; it is the greatest act of deliverance by God for His people, through Christ.

This life-altering salvation storyline is woven throughout Scripture. It's not only in the New Testament but starts at the very beginning and grows in intensity until the end.

Prophecy.

Foreshadowing.

Provision.

Fulfillment.

In other words, sin entered the world as man and woman listened to the lies of the serpent and followed their impulsive desires instead of God's clear commands. Therefore, the people remained in bondage and in need of a deliverer. At the right time, God sent Jesus to deliver them, and us, from the oppression of sin. Jesus crushed the head of the serpent so we could be restored to God.

Read Revelation 12:9–12 for the dramatic, vivid account of the enemy being thrown down! These verses declare Christ's ultimate victory and remind us that through His blood and the word of our testimony we triumph over the enemy. Hallelujah!

### The Rising of the Sun in Its Strength

Now it's time to finish up the testimony song. Judges 5:28–30 mentions Sisera's mother. Since Sisera had oppressed God's people for many years, under the leadership of Jabin, she was used to her son returning victoriously from his military conquests. But here she was perplexed, wondering why his horse and chariot were taking so long to return him safely to her. "Why is his chariot so long in coming? Why don't I hear the hoofbeats of his horses?" (v. 28). Sisera's mother even rationalized her son's delay; he and his troops were probably finding and dividing the spoils from the battle, each man taking a girl or two as a prize, and Sisera was probably swiping the colored garments for himself, even securing a fancy garment or two for her. But we know Sisera wasn't returning. He could no longer oppress God's people. He had been defeated once and for all.

Deborah's song concludes in verse 31: "LORD, may all your enemies perish as Sisera did. But may those who love [You] be like the rising of the sun in its strength." After the song is complete, there is one more sentence: "And the land had peace for forty years" (v. 31). *Selah.*

The enemy is defeated! We can experience peace—not only a momentary peace or a forty-year peace but a permanent peace—one beyond all understanding, one that does not flee in the face of challenging circumstances, one that lasts. How is this possible? It's because peace is not a mere feeling; it is Jesus, the Prince of Peace.

Our lives should look different from how they used to because of Jesus. When we encounter Him, He changes us from the inside out and makes us more like Him as we follow Him.

> Jesus is with you through it all—every misstep, every iron chariot, every flood, every battle, every rescue, every triumph.

Jesus is with you through it all—every misstep, every iron chariot, every flood, every battle, every rescue, every triumph. There is peace in His presence. He is meant to be shared with those around you. Don't be silent; sing and proclaim what Jesus has done. Don't hide the Good News from a hurting world. Acts 1:8 says, "But you will receive power when the Holy Spirit has come on you, and you will be my witnesses in Jerusalem, in all Judea and Samaria, and to the ends of the earth." Your testimony can be used by the power of the

Holy Spirit to help set others free from the bondage of sin. Point them to Jesus and entrust the results to Him.

## Reflect

1. Record what you learn about Jesus being our peace in the following Scriptures:

Isaiah 9:6–7

Ephesians 2:11–18

Colossians 3:15–17

2. Read Psalm 107:1–22. This psalm is a testimony of God's mercy and His steadfast love. Verse 2 says, "Let the redeemed of the LORD proclaim that he has redeemed them from the power of the foe." The English Standard Version says it like this: "Let the redeemed of the LORD say so." Use the space below to write a testimony about how God has provided for you or delivered you. Consider sharing this testimony with others so their faith can be strengthened too.

There are many testimonies I could share with you as we get ready to close this study. But I think it's fitting to conclude the story of my school board race. The journey started out as a reluctant yes to obey, coupled with a desperate SOS prayer: "God, I don't know how to do this, please show me and provide along this journey." God answered, faithfully directing my steps and providing in ways I never could have imagined. It is one of the hardest things I have done, requiring more faith, more patience, and more courage than I was capable of in my own strength. I met new friends along the way, and even witnessed several people come back to God throughout the process. I experienced the lavish gift of a group of people interceding for me and my family and showing their support in a thousand ways. It was a team effort. With God's help, I did my part and others did theirs, but mostly God did His. I didn't know what the results would be when the vote took place. I honestly had mixed feelings, knowing that if I was elected more hard work would begin, but I also wanted to offer hope to many who had lost it. Turns out, I received the most votes and was elected to the school board. Only God can part seas like that! The impossible is His specialty. I'm living proof.

My friend, you might be praying an SOS prayer of your own. "God, what do I do about _____?" You may be wondering how your current circumstance is going to work out. I don't have the specific answer to that, but I do know that God can be trusted; He acts faithfully, in love. Even when election results don't go your way, even when you get a no when you were counting on a yes, even when the conflicts in your home or the world make no earthly sense—God is the security and stability you need to navigate this life. He readily supplies the truth required to make wise decisions in uncertain times.

I am praying Psalm 107:43 over you as you finish this study and reflect on what God has revealed to you through His Word and His Spirit: "Let whoever is wise pay attention to these things and consider the LORD's acts of faithful love."

Let's offer thanksgiving to God for what He has done, giving Him the credit for delivering us from spiritual destruction and supplying us with endless hope now and into eternity. Let's rely on His power to fuel our faith as we decide to fully follow Him. May these lyrics be our prayer, our response, our resolve: "I have decided to follow Jesus. No turning back, no turning back."[2]

## Bonus

Read Psalm 107 and write down a few verses you want to remember or memorize from the psalm.

## DECIDE

When you experience peace, decide to give credit to God as you testify about what He has provided.

*Dear Jesus,*

*Increase my awe of You. May I not grow indifferent to Your majesty, Your wonders, and the intricacies of Your creation. You have done, are doing, and will do marvelous things. Thank You for protecting me, providing for me, and refining me. You never fail. You do not mess up or get it wrong. You are ready and waiting to restore me when I repent and turn from sin. Cast down my idols so that You are exalted. Take Your rightful place in my life. There is no thing and no one who compares with You. Give me the desire and motivation to live for You each day—a living sacrifice. Thank You that in You I have unending hope.*

*Give me courage to testify of Your love, to proclaim what You have done, and to pay attention to every answered prayer. Fill my heart with thanksgiving, my mind with truth, and my voice with praise. You are worthy to receive glory and honor and power, for You created all things, and because of Your will they existed and were created (Rev. 4:11). I choose to bow down to You alone. May I rejoice as I worship You. May I not keep silent but proclaim what You have done. Amen.*

# WEEK 5 WRAP-UP

*This week, I decide to testify of God's power,*
*His glorious deeds, and His mighty wonders.*

Answer the following questions to help summarize what you learned during this week of study. If possible, use biblical references to back up your responses.

1. What is a line from Deborah's song, in Judges 5, that stands out to you?

2. What did you learn about the importance of testifying of God's faithfulness, based on the Scriptures you read this week?

3. What is one of your favorite stories from the Bible or favorite songs that proclaims God's power and goodness?

4. Record a specific example from Scripture or from your own life for the following categories from Psalm 78:4.

Glorious deeds of the Lord:

His might:

The wonders He has done:

Now, tell someone younger than you what He has done based on your answers above.

5. Based on what you discovered in Lessons 1–5, how can the decision to testify help you make wise decisions in uncertain times?

# Conclusion

The most important decision you will ever make is deciding what to do with Jesus. Throughout this study, we have asked, "God, what do I do?" While that is a great question, take a minute and let God ask you a question: "What will you do with Jesus?"

Will you accept Him or reject Him?

In Acts 2, after the Holy Spirit had filled the disciples, Peter preached to the crowd gathered around them. Enabled by the Spirit, he explained numerous Scriptures and how they pointed to Jesus (from the prophet Joel and from King David). He connected the dots for those listening, compelling them to move from unbelief to belief. In verse 36, Peter said, "Therefore let all the house of Israel know with certainty that God has made this Jesus, whom you crucified, both Lord and Messiah." The listeners were "pierced to the heart" by this, and they asked Jesus's disciples, "Brothers, what should we do?" (v. 37).

Peter's answer in verse 38 provides a clear road map:

- Repent.
- Be baptized in the name of Jesus for the forgiveness of sins.
- Receive the gift of the Holy Spirit.

Peter explained in verse 39 that this promise was for those listening and for their children, for all those near and "all who are far off, as many as the Lord our God will call."

Whether you feel near to God or far off, the wisest decision you will ever make is to say yes to Jesus—to repent, be baptized in Jesus's name for the forgiveness of your sins, and receive the Holy Spirit. If you haven't yet taken these faith steps, I invite you to do so now.

═══════

As we conclude this study, let's review the wise decisions we can make in uncertain times. Here is an easy way to remember the first letter of each week's decision. When you don't know what to do, you can decide to be a ROBERT. Really? Ha! I promise I didn't plan that, but the first letters of our six weekly decisions spell out Robert, which led me on a brief search to see what the name Robert means. It's of German origin, and it means "bright fame." And somehow that is fitting, isn't it? When we are at a crossroads, when we are uncertain what to do next, we can't go wrong by shining brightly like the sun for God's fame, for His renown—following His ways and praising Him for His faithfulness to us. "May those who love him be like the rising of the sun in its strength" (Judg. 5:31).

When we find ourselves asking, "God, what do I do?" may we rely on the wisdom we discovered throughout Judges 1–5 and decide to:

**R**emember who Jesus is and what He has done.

**O**bey God's commands completely, not partially.

**B**e responsible with our thoughts, actions, and influence.

**E**ndure through the power of the Holy Spirit and the armor of God.

**R**ise in faith to fulfill our unique purpose at this time in history.

**T**estify of God's power, His glorious deeds, and His mighty wonders.

# Acknowledgments

Jesus: thank You for speaking clearly to me on Mount Precipice about studying and writing about Deborah. May I not steamroll or shrink back from Your call upon my life, even when the next step is uncertain. Help me to be found faithful to care for the people You've entrusted to me and carry out the projects You've given to me. No turning back. May You get the glory, praise, and thanks!

Adam: your support and patience astound me. Thank you for understanding this calling and for all you do to make room for this work. The way you love people and are committed to God's Word inspires me. Thank you for humoring me as I was flapping around with excitement, telling you about my "aha" moment about Jael.

Brooke, Kale, Banner, Isaiah, and Lark: this family and ministry are a team effort, and it did not go unnoticed how you sacrificed and stepped up so that these words could be written. I am proud to be your mom! It is my prayer that you keep following Jesus in every season. May your faith become your own as you stand upon the wisdom of His Word and lean into His strong, capable arms.

Central Church: I am grateful for this grace-filled place to grow and serve. God has, is, and will do marvelous things in our midst. Let's keep Jesus and people central through it all.

Mom and Dad: thank you for introducing me to Jesus through worship songs, Bible stories, attending church as a family, and your faith-filled example.

Jenaye Merida: thank you for representing me, thinking outside of the box, and championing this message of hope. I am grateful for your persistence, your encouragement, and this beautiful partnership.

Baker Books: thank you, Patnacia Goodman, for your enthusiasm in acquiring this project, and big thanks to Eddie LaRow for your reassurance, for encouraging me to rework it, and for seeing this project through from beginning to end. It was a joy to work with you! Much appreciation also to Brianna DeWitt, Rachel Hamlin, Chris Kuhatschek, Lindsey Spoolstra, Anne Van Solkema, and the entire Baker team for your dedication to excellence and to helping this study make a difference in the lives of many.

Beth Rubin: I'm thrilled to have your stunning photography on the cover.

Christina Custodio: thank you for the author photo and the belly laughs.

Kay Arthur: your commitment to studying and applying God's Word inductively has greatly impacted me. God has used Precept Bible Studies to shape, refine, and grow me.

Dr. Jeff Leonard: I am grateful for you leading our trip to Israel and for the wealth of knowledge you shared with us. Thank you for teaching me about Deborah and highlighting her story during our trip.

Kaitlyn Bouchillon: you were there with me on Mount Precipice, and you were probably the first one I whisper-told, "My next book is going to be about Deborah." Thank you for introducing me to the Holy Land.

Lee Nienhuis: your passion for Jesus and your devotion to spending time with Him are contagious. Thank you for pointing me back to the Bible, Jesus, and the gospel time and time again.

Jennifer Hand: thank you for cheering on this message and for saying the right thing when I was running out of steam. Thank you for praying for me at the Church of Annunciation. God writes amazing stories! Your "yes" life inspires me.

Janyre Tromp: thank you for helping me frame this message in a unique and cohesive way at the writing retreat. Your guiding questions helped unlock the perspective I needed to study Judges.

Nicole Homan: you inspire me to keep offering what's in my basket. I am grateful for your friendship, your example, and your love for Jesus.

Sarae Martin: thank you for teaching me how to study God's Word for myself. Your commitment to learning the truth and applying it has made such a difference.

Bill and Carolyn Wilkie: I am grateful for your willingness to send me to inductive Bible study training. I hope you enjoy the fruit of what you sowed all those years ago.

Laurie Wickes: thank you for your example, for asking great questions, and for being a dear friend.

Paula Stitt: I am grateful for your monthly mentoring calls and for your gifts of understanding and encouragement.

Randy Siedlecki and Christy Mobley: thank you for your willingness to read this through first. I appreciate your support.

Jessica Helwig: thank you for being one of the first ones to affirm the need for this content. It was fun to share the rough draft with you.

Tami Krohn and Amanda Johns: your encouragement came right on time. Thank you for valuing this project.

My AZ Gals: Janell Neumann, Tracy Steel, Carol Tetzlaff, and Erica Wiggenhorn—what a lineup of dynamos for the kingdom. Thank you for loving the Word and teaching the Word and for your friendship. Thanks also for sharing your state with me and for your encouragement.

Amber Lia and Erin Warren: big thanks for your prayers, your insight, and your friendship over the years.

Ministry prayer team: thank you for praying this study through to the finish line. God provided breakthroughs as you pressed in and covered this project in prayer.

Friday morning prayer group: your friendship is a gift; your prayers shake the ground!

Listeners of *The Martha + Mary Show*, admins and members of *The Martha + Mary Show* sisterhood, and subscribers of my "Good News-Letter": thank you for being a part of this growing community that wants to be "all in" for Jesus.

# Notes

**Week 1, Lesson 1  "God, What Do I Do First?"**

1. Adapted from Erica Wiggenhorn, keynote address, Speak Up Conference, Friday, July 8, 2022, Grand Rapids, Michigan.
2. "Strong's H7592—šā'al," Blue Letter Bible, accessed September 11, 2024, https://www.blueletterbible.org/lexicon/h7592/esv/wlc/0-1/.
3. C. S. Lewis, *The Horse and His Boy* (HarperCollins, 2002).
4. "Strong's H8085—šāmaʿ," Blue Letter Bible, accessed September 11, 2024, https://www.blueletterbible.org/lexicon/h8085/esv/wlc/0-1/.
5. Lois Tverberg, "Shema—Hear and Obey," En-Gedi Resource Center, June 30, 2015, https://engediresourcecenter.com/2015/06/30/shema-hear-and-obey.
6. Tverberg, "Shema—Hear and Obey."

**Week 1, Lesson 2  "God, What Do I Do When I Need Help?"**

1. "Matthew Henry's Commentary: Judges 1:1," Bible Hub, accessed July 21, 2022, https://biblehub.com/commentaries/mhc/judges/1.htm.

**Week 1, Lesson 3  "God, What Do I Do with What You've Given Me?"**

1. "Tel Arad National Park," Israel Nature and Parks Authority, accessed July 30, 2022, https://en.parks.org.il/reserve-park/tel-arad-national-park/.

**Week 1, Lesson 4  "God, What Do I Do When You Speak to Me?"**

1. Michael Rydelnik and Michael Vanlaningham, eds., *The Moody Bible Commentary* (Moody Publishers, 2014), 361.

**Week 2, Lesson 2  "God, What Do I Do with My Influence?"**

1. "Strong's H3045—yāḍaʿ," Blue Letter Bible, accessed September 11, 2024, https://www.blueletterbible.org/lexicon/h3045/csb/wlc/0-1/.
2. "The Chronology of Judges Solved!" Bible Archeology, accessed August 30, 2024, https://www.bible.ca/archeology/bible-archeology-exodus-route-date-chronology-of-judges.htm.
3. "Strong's G1097—ginōskō," Blue Letter Bible, accessed September 11, 2024, https://www.blueletterbible.org/lexicon/g1097/csb/mgnt/0-1/.

4. Rydelnik and Vanlaningham, *Moody Bible Commentary*, 361.

5. "Judges 5 Commentary: Judges 5:8," Precept Austin, accessed September 11, 2024, https://www.preceptaustin.org/judges_5_commentary#5:8.

### Week 2, Lesson 5  "God, What Do I Do When Life Feels Heavy?"

1. "Strong's g1242—diatheke," Blue Letter Bible, accessed September 11, 2024, https://www.blueletterbible.org/search/Dictionary/viewTopic.cfm?topic=VT0000601.

2. *Oxford Languages*, "atrophied," accessed September 11, 2024, https://www.google.com/search?q=atrophied+definition.

### Week 3, Lesson 1  "God, What Do I Do When I'm Tested?"

1. "Strong's G1515—eirēnē," Blue Letter Bible, accessed September 13, 2024, https://www.blueletterbible.org/lexicon/g1515/kjv/tr/0-1/.

2. Rosilind Jukic, "7 Weapons for Spiritual Warfare—Free Printable!" A Little R&R Writings, July 11, 2022, https://rosilindjukic.com/spiritual-weapons-battle-is-long/.

### Week 3, Lesson 2  "God, What Do I Do When I'm in a Battle?"

1. Matthew Henry, *Matthew Henry's Commentary on the Whole Bible*, vol. 2, *Joshua–Esther* (Fleming H. Revell, 1975), 133. Emphasis in original.

### Week 3, Lesson 4 "God, What Do I Do When I Experience Opposition?"

1. J. R. R. Tolkien, *The Fellowship of the Ring* (Houghton Mifflin, 1954), 322.

### Week 3, Lesson 5  "God, What Do I Do Next?"

1. "What Is an Ox Goad? Let Wisdom Be Our Goad," YouTube video, 10:02, uploaded by Spirit & Truth, February 8, 2010, https://youtu.be/NJXy2uqq6s4.

2. Henry, *Matthew Henry's Commentary on the Whole Bible*, 2:138.

### Week 4, Lesson 1  "God, What Do I Do When I'm Worried?"

1. Rydelnik and Vanlaningham, *Moody Bible Commentary*, 367.

2. "Strong's H1683—dᵉḇôrâ," Blue Letter Bible, accessed September 13, 2024, https://www.blueletterbible.org/lexicon/h1683/kjv/wlc/0-1/.

3. Rydelnik and Vanlaningham, *Moody Bible Commentary*, 361.

4. Henry, *Matthew Henry's Commentary on the Whole Bible*, 2:138.

### Week 4, Lesson 2  "God, What Do I Do When I'm Intimidated?"

1. Sam Storms, "What Does Scripture Teach About the Office of Prophet and Gift of Prophecy?," The Gospel Coalition, October 8, 2015, www.thegospelcoalition.org/article/sam-storms-what-does-scripture-teach-about-office-prophet-gift-prophecy/.

2. Rydelnik and Vanlaningham, *Moody Bible Commentary*, 368.

3. Rydelnik and Vanlaningham, *Moody Bible Commentary*, 368.

### Week 4, Lesson 3  "God, What Do I Do When I Feel Alone?"

1. "I Have Decided to Follow Jesus—1 Popular Hymn by Sadhu Sundar Singh," Bibilium, accessed August 29, 2024, https://bibilium.com/i-have-decided-to-follow-jesus-sadhu-sundar-singh/.

**Week 4, Lesson 4  "God, What Do I Do When I'm Bombarded by Lies?"**

1. If you'd like to hear more about Jaelle's story, listen to my interview with her mom, Cherri Bornman, in "Episode 156: Miracles in the Waiting Room," *The Martha + Mary Show*, December 21, 2022, available wherever you get your podcasts or at https://www.katiemreid .com/2022/12/miracles-waiting-room-cherri-bornman/.

2. Adapted from "Excerpts from *Manner and Customs of Bible Lands* by Fred H. Wight," Ancient Hebrew Research Center, accessed September 17, 2024, https://www.ancient-hebrew .org/manners/the-sacred-duty-of-hospitality.htm.

3. Henry, *Matthew Henry's Commentary on the Whole Bible*, 2:144.

4. Henry, *Matthew Henry's Commentary on the Whole Bible*, 2:144.


**Week 4, Lesson 5  "God, What Do I Do When Enemies Rise Against Me?"**

1. See "Westminster Shorter Catechism: Q1," Bible Presbyterian Church General Synod, accessed September 18, 2024, https://www.shortercatechism.com/resources/wsc/wsc_001 .html.


**Week 5, Lesson 1  "God, What Do I Do When I've Been Delivered?"**

1. Rydelnik and Vanlaningham, *Moody Bible Commentary*, 368.

2. Rydelnik and Vanlaningham, *Moody Bible Commentary*, 368.

3. "Judges 5 Notes: Songs of Deliverance by C H Spurgeon," Precept Austin, accessed September 18, 2024, https://www.preceptaustin.org/judges_5_notes#sod.


**Week 5, Lesson 2  "God, What Do I Do to Encourage Those Around Me?"**

1. "Judges 5 Commentary: Judges 5:8," Precept Austin, accessed October 16, 2024, https://www.preceptaustin.org/judges_5_commentary#5:8.

2. "Episode 107: Telling Your Story," *The Martha + Mary Show*, September 15, 2021, available wherever you get your podcasts or at https://www.katiemreid.com/2021/09/telling -your-story-kate-motaung/.


**Week 5, Lesson 3  "God, What Do I Do When Someone Has Let Me Down?"**

1. Oxford Languages, "flattery," accessed September 18, 2024, https://www.google.com /search?q=flattery+definition.


**Week 5, Lesson 4  "God, What Do I Do When I'm Outnumbered?"**

1. Bob Deffinbaugh, "What in the World Is Going On? A Study of God's Plan for Man: 4. Nature's Part in God's Perfect Plan (Psalm 19; Romans 8:18–25; Isaiah 65:17–25)," Bible .org, accessed September 18, 2024, https://bible.org/seriespage/4-natures-part-gods-perfect -plan-psalm-19-romans-818-25-isaiah-6517-25.

2. "Judges 5: Matthew Poole's Commentary," Bible Hub, accessed September 18, 2024, https://biblehub.com/commentaries/poole/judges/5.htm.

3. Excerpted from Katie M. Reid, "The God Who Helps You: Psalm 121," *She Lives Fearless* (blog), August 24, 2022, https://shelivesfearless.com/the-god-who-helps-you-psalm-121/.


**Week 5, Lesson 5  "God, What Do I Do When I Experience Peace?"**

1. Henry, *Matthew Henry's Commentary on the Whole Bible*, 2:151.

2. Bibilium, "I Have Decided to Follow Jesus."

**KATIE M. REID** is a dynamic speaker, podcast host of *The Martha + Mary Show*, and author of the book and Bible study *Made Like Martha*. She teaches at retreats and events and serves on faculty at writing and speaking conferences. Discovering "aha" moments in the Bible, enjoying sunrises and sunsets, and inspiring others to live out their God-given purpose are some of her favorite things to do. Katie and her family live in Michigan. Connect at Katie MReid.com and subscribe to Katie's monthly "Good News-Letter."

## CONNECT WITH KATIE

KatieMReid.com

 @KatieMReidWriter

 @Katie_M_Reid

 @Katie_M_Reid